Advance P

"In this important book, Mike Strain persuasively bolsters his title claim that 'the American Dream is not dead.' While the nation faces disruptive challenges from economic changes from trade and technology, those very changes help propel our prosperity. What could kill the American Dream, as Strain notes, is a populist call for protection. Every serious student of the current economic and political situation should read this book."

—GLENN HUBBARD, dean emeritus and Russell
L. Carson Professor of Finance and Economics, Columbia
Business School, and former chairman of the
Council of Economic Advisers

"Before you declare the American Dream is dead, you should take the time to read Michael Strain's case to the contrary. Strain provides a thoughtful and balanced assessment of the evidence on the state of American workers and families, in the process rejecting some of the claims coming from both the left and the right."

—JASON FURMAN, professor of practice, Harvard Kennedy School and former chairman of the
Council of Economic Advisers

"Michael Strain is one of the keenest economists at work on the center-right today. In this brief but important book, he dares to bring facts to the overheated and often poorly informed debate over the state of the American Dream. Engaging and convincing, it is essential reading for anyone who wants to understand our economic present—and future."

—Rich Lowry, editor of *National Review*

"In this lively contribution to our national debate, Michael Strain presents the evidence for how Americans are really doing. Strain shows we're faring better than you'd think from doom-sayers of left and right. He also argues that misunderstanding our real situation could lead to foolish and damaging policies that would make things worse, not better. An important short book."

—William Kristol, director, Defending Democracy Together

"This vital book suggests we reconsider the doom and gloom economic narrative, in favor of acknowledging that ongoing economic progress continues to deliver rising material prosperity each year, increasing opportunity, and greater freedom from want. The argument matters, because the strongest foundation for a 'small c' conservative perspective is that a system that delivers such progress is worth conserving. Strain's intellectual depth, policy breadth, and relentless honesty mark him as one of the leading conservative intellectuals of our time. I'm no conservative, partly because I might see the case for change more clearly than Strain. But Strain asks hard questions, presents uncomfortable data, and makes counterarguments more clearly than any other right-of-center wonk. Whatever side of politics you're on, this smart little book will make you a better wonk, with a clearer sense about the facts that underpin the biggest policy debates of our time."

—JUSTIN WOLFERS, professor of economics and public policy, University of Michigan

"Just how good or bad are things in America right now? Michael Strain's *The American Dream Is Not Dead* is the most balanced and informative take on this question you are likely to see."

—TYLER COWEN, professor of economics, George Mason University and coauthor of the *Marginal Revolution* blog

"The American Dream is alive and well—not based on wishful thinking, but on an abundance of evidence. Michael Strain's balanced and expert presentation, acknowledging problems but identifying the strengths in America's economy, is exactly what the policy debate has needed: a data-driven look at good news that has been ignored by politicians of left and right alike."

—CHARLES MURRAY, F. A. Hayek Chair, American Enterprise Institute

"While I'm not convinced that the American Dream is entirely healthy, I'm more optimistic about its prospects after reading this book. I'm regularly on the other side of an argument from Michael Strain, yet I crave reading what he writes, because in it I'll find more compelling reasoning than I'll typically otherwise encounter. Michael's willingness to engage constructively and convincingly makes him an important voice in any meaningful discussion about the American Dream."

—ALI VELSHI, host, MSNBC

"Michael Strain's *The American Dream Is Not Dead* should be read widely by people who think—or fear—otherwise. In clear and simple style, this accessible, no-nonsense treatise lays out the basic facts about the track record of the American economy, and how the economy has delivered for ordinary Americans by such yardsticks as wage growth, middle class job creation, family income, and economic mobility. By these and other criteria, he argues, performance in recent decades has been tolerably good—certainly much better than many of us have been told."

—NICHOLAS EBERSTADT, Henry Wendt Chair in Political Economy, American Enterprise Institute

"We have a bad news bias. Frequently, however, that creates an inaccurate picture of the world. In *The American Dream Is Not Dead*, Michael Strain shows that while there are very real challenges ahead of us as a country, Americans are living in the best, most prosperous time in our nation's history. This book shows that hope and truth go together."

—ARTHUR C. BROOKS, professor of practice, Harvard Kennedy School & Arthur C. Patterson Faculty Fellow, Harvard Business School

The American Dream Is Not Dead

THE AMERICAN DREAM IS NOT DEAD

(But Populism Could Kill It)

Michael R. Strain

TEMPLETON PRESS

Templeton Press
300 Conshohocken State Road, Suite 500
West Conshohocken, PA 19428
www.templetonpress.org

Set in Sabon LT Pro 9.9/14.4 by Gopa&Ted2, Inc.

Library of Congress Control Number: 2020930637

ISBN: 978-1-59947-557-8 (paperback: alk. paper)
ISBN: 978-1-59947-558-5 (ebook)

This paper meets the requirements of ANSI/NISO Z39.48-1992
(Permanence of Paper).
A catalogue record for this book is available
from the Library of Congress.

20 21 22 23 24   10 9 8 7 6 5 4 3 2 1

Printed in the United States of America.

For William and Rose

Contents

———— ≥≤ ————

The American Dream Is Not Dead

Introduction

——————— ≳≲ ———————

THE AMERICAN DREAM is not dead.

It is surprising that such a sentence would be so controversial. But it is. If you're looking for bipartisan consensus, start here. Leading politicians and presidential candidates from both parties have voiced agreement on these points: America is no longer an upwardly mobile society. Incomes are stagnant. Workers don't enjoy the fruits of their labor. Typical households are no better off today than they were decades ago. The game is rigged for everyone but those at the top.

It is always difficult to capture the reality of American life in short sentences. A country as large as ours, in which citizens have such varied experiences, makes generalizing difficult. But today's prevailing narrative is so stark that the task of generalizing becomes much easier. The narrative is wrong. America is upwardly mobile, particularly for those nearer the bottom of the income distribution. Incomes aren't stagnant. Workers do enjoy the fruits of their labor. The argument that life hasn't improved for typical households in decades borders on the absurd. The game is not rigged.

The American Dream is not dead. And this short book will hopefully convince you of that.

My goal here is not to be Panglossian. I believe that if a glass is one-tenth full, it's better to describe it as nine-tenths empty. My argument is that if the American Dream were a glass, it's much closer to full than to empty.

My goal is also not to be contrarian. The United States faces serious economic challenges, including managing the effects of advancing technology, declining workforce participation rates, towns and communities that have been left behind by globalization, failing schools, tempered dynamism and energy, and relatively slow productivity growth. America faces serious social challenges as well, including decaying social capital, increasing socioeconomic fragmentation, "deaths of despair," the opioid crisis, and a very troubling increase in suicides.

But despite these very real challenges, the national conversation about the American Dream is so detached from the underlying reality that it has become incorrect. We are confusing pockets of real struggle in American life with the broader canvas of the American experience.

This confusion matters because messages matter. What people believe about their ability to improve their economic lot affects their aspirations, motivation, and effort in the labor market, which in turn affects their economic outcomes.

The message people receive today from politicians and opinion leaders is that hard work won't pay off, incomes won't grow, and they can't climb up the ladder. That message is unfair to the people who are receiving it precisely because it is wrong. The message helps to create the very problems its advocates argue exist.

This is not a call to complacency. The American Dream always needs to be renewed because every generation faces different social and economic challenges. In addition to the serious issues I mentioned above, the Dream is at immediate risk from populists on the left and the right—from their policies, from their narratives of victimhood and grievance, and from their assaults on the value of personal responsibility and the idea that people can better their outcomes.

The American people deserve better than a populist scream. They deserve policies that strengthen the Dream, advance economic opportunity, and increase economic mobility. That debate should take place in the afternoon sun, not in the darkness of midnight. It's not midnight in America. But it could be brighter still.

Part I

The American Dream Is Not Dead

CHAPTER 1

Defining the Dream

——————— ≥≤ ———————

WHAT IS the American Dream? It means different things to different people, of course, and its meaning has changed over time. For many, individual liberty is essential to the American Dream. So is having a good family and a strong community. Homeownership is an important component, as is a comfortable retirement. (To illustrate the breadth and variety of its definition, consider that the *New York Times* recently asserted, "Well-manicured lawns have long been a symbol" of the American Dream.[1])

My American Enterprise Institute (AEI) colleagues Samuel Abrams, Karlyn Bowman, Eleanor O'Neil, and Ryan Streeter commissioned a survey published in February 2019 that asks about the American Dream.[2] Ninety-four percent of respondents reported that having a successful career was essential or important to their own view of the Dream. Eighty-eight percent reported the same about having a better quality of life than their parents.

I mention these two items because of the strong economic component at play in the American Dream. At its core, economic success is one of the most important parts of the Dream. This doesn't mean achieving fabulous wealth, of course. Instead, it means a chicken in every pot. If you work hard and play by the rules, you can get ahead. Your effort will be rewarded. America is a place where you can build a better life for yourself and, in an economic sense, where your children will be better off than you. And in America, going from rags to riches is still possible.

This component of the Dream is the focus of this little book—not because the political and community components are unimportant—but because the economic component is so central, and—importantly—because it is the focus of today's misguided narrative.

———— ❊ ————

CHAPTER 2

Today's Message: The Dream Is Dead

THAT MISGUIDED NARRATIVE sends a clear message: The American Dream is dead. There is no room for nuance in the message our political leaders are sending. This message is fueled in large part by an effort to understand and react to the emergence of populism in both political parties. Let's look at a few quick examples, of many.

President Trump has been arrestingly clear on this point, stating directly, in June 2015: "Sadly, the American Dream is dead."[3] In May 2016, Senator Bernie Sanders said, "American workers are some of the most overworked yet our standard of living has fallen. For many, the American Dream has become a nightmare."[4]

In a December 2018 essay in *The Atlantic*, Senator Marco Rubio wrote, "There was once a path to a stable and prosperous life in America that has since closed off. It was a well-traveled path for many Americans: Graduate from high school and get a job, typically with a local manufacturer or one of the service industries associated with it and earn enough to support a family. The idea was not only that it was possible to achieve this kind of success, but that anyone could achieve it—the American Dream. That dream defines my family's history, and its disappearance calls me to action today."[5]

In the spring of 2015, Senator Elizabeth Warren and Mayor Bill de Blasio wrote, "Across generations, Americans shared the belief that hard work would bring opportunity and a better life. America wasn't perfect, but we invested in our kids and put in place policies to build a strong middle class. We don't do that anymore, and the result is clear: The rich get richer, while everyone else falls behind. The game is rigged, and the people who rigged it want it to stay that way."[6]

While giving the commencement address at The King's College in the spring of 2019, freshman U.S. senator Joshua Hawley, Republican from Missouri, told graduates that "if you don't have family wealth, and if you don't have a four-year degree—and that's 70 percent of Americans. Seventy percent—the future is far less glowing. These Americans haven't seen a real wage increase in thirty years."[7]

This pessimistic view is pervasive, and it extends to commentators, public intellectuals, and business leaders. For example, Fox News host Tucker Carlson declared in January 2019 that "the American Dream is dying," and referred to "the dark age that we are living through."[8] The economist Joseph Stiglitz, Nobel laureate and former chair of the Council of Economic Advisers, recently wrote that "the

American economy is failing its citizens."[9] Ray Dalio, the billionaire founder of investment firm Bridgewater Associates, wrote a long essay posted on LinkedIn in the spring of 2019, critiquing American capitalism and offering reforms. When discussing the essay on *60 Minutes*, Dalio was as blunt as these elected leaders and presidential candidates: "I think the American Dream is lost."[10]

The American Dream is not lost.

CHAPTER 3

We Have Real Challenges

— ❯❮ —

B UT THIS is not to say that we don't face real challenges. Of course we do—in our politics, economy, and culture. Political polarization, tribalism, and excessive partisanship are very real and damaging. The emergence of the political entertainment establishment reduces politics of its seriousness, often misinforms the public, and inflames passions in a way that is destructive.

The rate at which prime-age men participate in the workforce has been falling for decades (figure 1). The participation of prime-age women has stagnated over the past two decades and seems in danger of declining as well. This is deeply troubling. Its macroeconomic implications are significant: A workforce that isn't growing will depress the growth of household income and living standards. On a social level, men without work are often men up to no good. Joblessness is correlated with crime, incarceration, and idleness. And for many individuals, a lack of employment makes it harder to be a good father and to get and stay married. For many, work is about more than a paycheck. It is how we contribute to society—and, importantly, how we can (correctly) be made to feel that we are contributing. It is a cure for boredom, which is one of the worst parts of life in a safe, modern, comfortable society. Work creates community. It emancipates us from our passions by directing them to productive ends.

FIGURE 1. PRIME-AGE LABOR FORCE PARTICIPATION RATE.

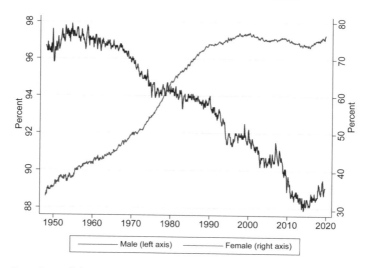

Source: Bureau of Labor Statistics; author's calculations.

Properly understood, work is deeply spiritual. Pope John Paul II wrote that man is "called to work." "Man is the image of God," wrote the late Pope, "partly through the mandate received from his Creator to subdue, to dominate, the earth. In carrying out this mandate, man, every human being, reflects the very action of the Creator of the universe." John Paul pointed out that we find "in the very first pages of the Book of Genesis" the "conviction that work is a fundamental dimension of human existence on earth."[11]

Our economic challenges are hardly limited to workforce participation. Technological advances and the automation of job tasks have been changing the labor market in significant ways for several decades and will continue to do so. This change has proven to be very disruptive and will likely be more so in the years ahead. Our schools are not up to the challenge of imparting skills that allow young people to command high wages in the twenty-first-century economy. Globalization has presented challenges to some towns and communities as well, which, along with automation, has reduced employment opportunities in some formerly prosperous locales.

In addition to adding workers, the other way to grow living standards over time is through increases in worker productivity. And productivity growth has been lackluster for many years.

These challenges have all received quite a lot of attention, so I won't dwell on them here. Let me mention one that hasn't gotten its due. Troublingly (and not just because they are likely contributing to slower productivity growth), business dynamism and entrepreneurship have been on the decline as well, and labor markets have become less fluid.

FIGURE 2: STARTUP RATE FOR PRIVATE U.S. FIRMS IN THE NONFARM SECTOR.

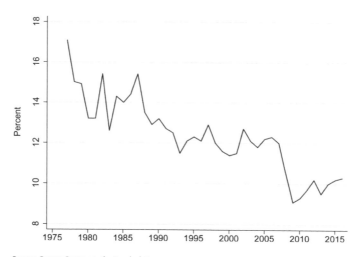

Source: Census Bureau; author's calculations.

The U.S. economy has been successful at generating economic opportunity in part because it has been successful at moving capital and workers to their most productive use. But business startups have been declining for years (figure 2). This is significant because young firms are a key driver of job creation and innovation.

The reallocation of workers across jobs often reflects career advancement and can improve the quality of the match between workers and firms, which increases workers' skills, productivity, and wages. The reallocation of jobs across businesses is another important indicator of fluidity and dynamism. Economists John Haltiwanger and Steven J. Davis document that both have been in decline for the last two decades (figure 3).

FIGURE 3. QUARTERLY RATES OF JOB REALLOCATION, WORKER REALLOCATION, AND CHURNING FOR THE U.S. NONFARM PRIVATE SECTOR, 1990Q2 TO 2013Q4.

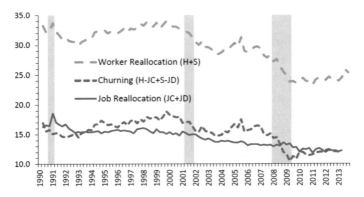

Source: Steven J. Davis and John Haltiwanger, "Labor Market Fluidity and Economic Performance," National Bureau of Economic Research Working Paper Series, no. w20479, 2014.

There are downsides to labor market dynamism, of course. And there can be benign and even positive effects of reduced dynamism. But I am troubled by these trends. Reduced fluidity suppresses productivity growth and wages and may even reduce overall employment.[12] These trends seem to be related to an overall reduction of restlessness and energy in American life. This manifests itself, for example, in a decline in people's willingness to pack up the car and move to a new city, and in the general sense that as a society we have become more risk averse. And it exacerbates economic disparities between regions of the country—specifically, between booming coastal urban centers and struggling rural and industrial areas. These regional disparities have animated and inflamed populist sentiment.

My intention is not to provide an exhaustive accounting of the economic challenges facing the United States, but instead to highlight several about which I am particularly concerned, and to make clear that we do face serious and difficult issues.

The same is true in American culture and social life. Robert Putnam, the Social Capital Project—an initiative of the Joint Economic Committee of the U.S. Congress started by Senator Mike Lee and led by social scientist Scott Winship—and my AEI colleagues Charles Murray, Tim Carney, Ryan Streeter, and Yuval Levin are just a few of many analysts and authors who are rightly concerned about the state of American associational life, the institutions of civil society, and the extent of socioeconomic segregation and fragmentation.

The opioid crisis and "deaths of despair"—a phrase coined in the important work of economists Anne Case and Angus Deaton—have been much discussed, and their rise has been deeply alarming.

The broader conversation about our cultural and social challenges can often be squishy, and one is reasonably left to wonder whether the troubles that many point out are really all that bad. There is much concern, for example, about an epidemic of loneliness sweeping the country. But how good is the data on loneliness? And isn't loneliness part of the human condition? There is much concern about the rise of a stay-at-home culture. But perhaps it is simply more enjoyable to order takeout and watch Netflix with your spouse than to go to dinner and a movie with friends. And, if so, what's the problem?

I don't intend to take a firm stand on those questions. But what has convinced me that many people are suffering is data on suicides. For the last ten years, more Americans of all ages have died by suicide than by car accident (figure 4).

FIGURE 4. DEATHS AMONG AMERICANS OF ALL AGES.

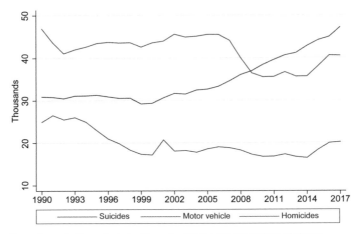

Source: Centers for Disease Control and Prevention, Fatal Injury Reports; author's calculations.

That trend line is clearly a problem and reflects even broader problems in our culture and society. The last decade in particular has been very hard on many individuals, and on American society as a whole. Our social challenges should not be minimized. But they should also not be treated as evidence of an overarching general decline.

CHAPTER 4

The American Dream Is Not Dead

≥≤

Despite these very real political, economic, and social and cultural challenges, the national conversation about the American Dream is sufficiently detached from the underlying reality that a corrective is in order. The basic narrative about the state of the American Dream is incorrect.

This is not to deny those challenges—including, but certainly not limited to, those previously discussed—or to suggest that they are overblown. Instead, my goal is to zoom out from these pockets of real struggle and attempt to characterize some important features of the broader picture. The broader picture is the more accurate reflection of the state of the country, and of the American Dream.

Yes, many towns left behind by automation and globalization are struggling. But most towns are not former manufacturing towns. Yes, male workers who never finished high school have seen their wages stagnate. But this has not been the experience for typical workers. Yes, far too many Americans are suffering from opioid addiction. But most

Americans are not. Yes, the recovery from the Great Recession was long and slow—agonizingly long for many. But the recession is in the rearview mirror.

Bruce Springsteen's songs are brilliant and moving. But most of us aren't characters in a Springsteen song.

In an effort to make sense of and react to the rise of populism on the political right and left, the national conversation has focused on our problems—groups that are struggling, places that are struggling, the causes and consequences of those struggles. This focus is helpful, of course, because politics and policy should be attuned to these issues. But we must remember that America is doing better than our biggest problems.

Specifically:

▶ Today's economy is delivering for American workers.
▶ Wages and incomes have not been stagnant for typical workers over the past three decades.
▶ The broader quality of life has improved significantly for typical households over the past several decades.
▶ Middle-income jobs have been "hollowed out," but a new middle of the labor market seems to be forming. And, in the aggregate, hollowing out is a story of middle-skill employment being replaced by high-skill employment.
▶ America is still broadly characterized by upward economic mobility.

Moreover, the message that the opposite of these statements is true is likely damaging. Precisely because hard work pays off and people can successfully climb the economic ladder, telling people that they cannot hurts their outcomes by sapping their energy and diminishing their aspirations.

CHAPTER 5

Today's Economy Is Delivering

≥≤

THE 2020 presidential campaign is at a boil, and populist unrest in both U.S. political parties has sparked a debate on capitalism. Trumpian populists and their sympathizers urge conservatives to put capitalism in its proper place— that is, to care less about "elite-serving" free markets and more about, say, the industrial policies and protectionism that they mistakenly believe will serve the interests of the working class. Populists on the left are pitting "the people" against "the elites" as well, inflaming angst and frustration, and calling for tax policy to target the wealthiest and for a wide range of new working-class and middle-class entitlement programs.

It's easy to see that this is at least in large part a reaction to the Great Recession and the slow recovery from it. Even still, given the state of the U.S. economy, it's an odd time for U.S. politicians to be questioning whether capitalism is broken.

The last month in which the economy lost more jobs than it gained was September 2010. Since then, the economy has added about 200,000 jobs each month. This steady progress has pushed total U.S. employment to its highest level on record as of the winter of 2019 (the time of this writing).

Fewer than four out of every 100 workers who wants a job cannot find one. The unemployment rate is lower than it has been since 1969. Today's economy is remarkably good at ensuring that workers who want a job can find a job.

For several years following the Great Recession, wages were growing at a disappointing rate. But wage growth is finally accelerating, with growth above 3 percent—and climbing. And over the past four years, median usual weekly nominal earnings have grown by 14 percent.

The rate at which people in their prime working years— ages 25 to 54; workers who are too old to be in school and too young to be retiring—participate in the workforce peaked in the late 1990s and fell until 2015. Since then, it has increased by 2.2 percentage points, erasing half a decade of decline.

At its peak following the Great Recession, there were over six unemployed workers for every job opening in the U.S. economy. Today, there are more job openings than there are unemployed workers.

One of the most troubling parts of the Great Recession and its aftermath was the large number of long-term unemployed workers (figure 5). These workers were willing to work, able to work, and actively looking for work without success for over six months. They were banging on doors and handing out résumés for month after month after month, unable to find a job.

FIGURE 5. LONG-TERM UNEMPLOYMENT RATE.

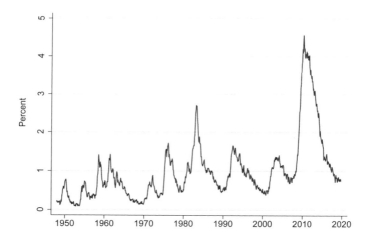

The long-term unemployment rate is the share of the labor force unemployed for 27 weeks or longer.
Source: Bureau of Labor Statistics data retrieved from FRED; author's calculations.

Being unemployed for so long is likely bad for your future in the labor market. It is obviously a blow to your lifetime income. But it is worse than that. The social and psychological effects can be devastating.

Ten months after the Great Recession officially ended, long-term unemployment peaked at 6.8 million workers. There are 82 percent fewer such workers at the time of this writing—fewer than when the Great Recession began.

Today's economy is delivering particularly well for the lowest-earning households. Usual weekly (nominal) earnings for workers for the bottom 10 percent have grown by 20 percent over the past four years—over one-third faster than growth at the median. The unemployment rate for workers without a high school diploma has dropped by over 10 percentage points from its post–Great Recession peak. It is further below its long-term average than the unemployment rate for college-educated workers.

The economy is also delivering for vulnerable workers. In January 2014, about 16 out of every 100 people with a disability had a job. In the winter of 2019, 19 out of 100 did—a 23 percent increase. With unemployment as low as it currently is, employers become much more flexible about which applicants they interview and hire. There are plenty of anecdotes that show what is likely happening systematically throughout the labor market. In April 2019, the *New York Times* reported that restaurants were "hiring former prisoners as kitchen assistants" due to the tight labor market.[13] Burning Glass Technologies, a company that analyzes the labor market, reported recently that employers have been increasingly unlikely to require background checks in their job postings.[14]

All is not perfect with the U.S. economy, of course. At any given time there are longer-term, slower-burning trends shaping economic fortunes, as well as shorter-term fluctuations around those trends. An economy doing great is not inconsistent with an economy that faces serious longer-term challenges, including, for example, disruption from technological automation, weak productivity growth, and schools that aren't adequately providing skills to tomorrow's workers.

But today's experience does tell us that a hot economy accrues to the benefit of everyone, including the lowest-income households and least-skilled workers. It accrues to the benefit of vulnerable workers.

Today's economy should inspire confidence in capitalism.

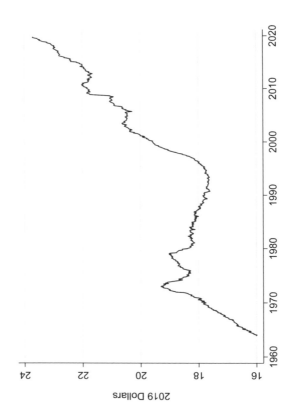

FIGURE 6. AVERAGE REAL WAGE FOR PRODUCTION AND NONSUPERVISORY EMPLOYEES.

Average hourly earnings for production and nonsupervisory employees adjusted for inflation using the personal consumption expenditures price index.

Source: Bureau of Labor Statistics and Bureau of Economic Analysis data retrieved from FRED; author's calculations.

CHAPTER 6
Incomes Are Growing

— ⋈ —

"WAGES FOR WORKERS except those at the top have been stagnant for decades." This assertion, or some variant of it, is extremely common. This claim is more wrong than right.

Instead, wages for typical workers have risen by 34 percent over the past three decades (figure 6). That's much less than the increase enjoyed by the top 1 percent, of course. But it is a significant increase in purchasing power, and this growth is not reasonably described as stagnant.

WAGES IN TEXTBOOK ECONOMIC THEORY

The textbook theory of wages is helpful and illuminating in understanding their real-world behavior. Workers enter the labor market because they need earnings in order to purchase goods and services. Firms enter the labor market because they need workers in order to produce goods and services. Workers supply labor in exchange for wages; firms demand labor services and pay wages for them.

The labor market is assumed to be competitive, which implies that no one firm can influence the market wage. So firms take the wage paid to workers as a given. Embedded in this framework is the assumption that each additional worker hired generates less revenue than workers hired previously. In this simple model, firms hire workers up to the point that the wage rate it pays is equal to the additional revenue the last worker generates for the firm. In other words, the firm hires workers until the additional cost the firm incurs for hiring its last worker (the wage rate) equals the additional revenue generated by the last worker.

The higher the wage, the more people who want to enter the labor market as workers, and the fewer people firms want to hire. At lower wages, fewer people want to work, but firms want to hire relatively more workers. The market settles on an equilibrium wage rate at which every firm can hire as many workers as it wants (knowing it has to pay the equilibrium wage) and every worker who wants to work (for the equilibrium wage) can find a job. The labor market clears. Labor supply equals labor demand.

This model leaves out quite a bit. Importantly, in actual labor markets, firms have some control over the wages they pay their workers. Wages may need to be higher than the "equilibrium market wage" in order to induce workers to switch employers or move to a new city. More broadly, mobility costs—the time, money, and effort required to switch jobs—give employers some power over wages by, for example, keeping wages below the market level for workers who don't want to incur the cost of switching jobs.

Firms that have a hard time monitoring their workers might pay higher wages to make slacking off and being fired relatively more costly. A firm might increase its workers' pay in order to make them more productive with the hope of retaining its existing workforce and reducing turnover, recruitment, and training costs. Wages are in part the result of a bargaining process between workers and firms as well.

The textbook model assumes that workers won't be paid less than the revenue they bring in to their employer because if they were, they would go down the street and get another job. But this assumes that workers have a good sense of what they're worth, and that they know what they could earn elsewhere. Imperfect information, then, can give firms power in markets over wages.

Institutions also affect wages. In the summer of 2018, more than a dozen major restaurant chains—including McDonald's and Applebee's—changed their contracts with franchisees to remove restrictions on workers in one franchise from getting a job at another franchise in the same chain.[15] These "no-poaching agreements" are actually very common in the low-wage labor market,[16] and they may lower wages by reducing the job options available to workers. "Noncompete agreements" are similar and restrict, for some period of time, workers from leaving one job and joining a competitor. Evidence suggests that one-fifth of all workers, including lower-income workers, are covered by a noncompete agreement.[17] (The actual importance of no-poaching and noncompete agreements to labor market outcomes like employment and wages is the subject of active research.)

Minimum wage regulation is a classic example of an institution that affects wages. Occupational licensing requirements are another important regulation. A recent study finds that the interstate migration rate for workers in occupations with state-specific licensing requirements is over one-third lower than for workers in other occupations.[18] Unions have historically been a very important labor market institution as well.

These real-world considerations are critically important. But they don't erase a central conclusion of the basic theory of wages: that to a first approximation they are determined by productivity.

Mobility costs and incomplete information are much stronger forces in the short run than they are over a longer period of time. It's harder to switch jobs tomorrow than it is to switch jobs sometime in the next few years. It's hard to know how much value you are providing to a firm today, but over time you get a better sense. Many middle-aged workers—with kids in school, who own homes and have roots in a community—may not be eager to pack up the car and move to a new city. But every year a new cohort of young people enter the labor market who are very mobile.

Intuitively, productivity should be a key determinant of wages. If a worker can only produce, say, $12 per hour of revenue, then why would his employer pay him $15 per hour over any length of time?

There is a limit to how far a business can push its wages below those being offered elsewhere in the market. That business will find its workers increasingly averse to putting in a hard day's work and will find it increasingly difficult to hire and retain workers. Market forces are very influential in real-world business decisions.

It's best to think of wages as being determined by a combination of institutions in the labor market, the relative bargaining power of workers and firms, and competitive market forces. Productivity is the baseline against which wages are set, and deviations from that baseline occur regularly.

WHICH WORKERS?
AND HOW TO ADJUST FOR INFLATION?

Over the next few pages, I present some evidence on how wages have evolved over time, and on the link between pay and productivity. There are two important considerations at the outset: Which workers do we care about? And how should we adjust for inflation?

Much of the policy discussion is focused on whether changes in the wages of *typical* workers are strongly connected to changes in macroeconomic productivity—the idea here is to see if typical workers are enjoying the fruits of overall productivity growth—and whether the wages of *typical* workers have been stagnant over time.

To study this, you could look at the wages of the median worker. That's the worker in the middle; half of all workers have higher wages than him, and half of all workers have lower wages than him.

You could also look at the average wage of production and nonsupervisory employees. They can be thought of as workers, not managers. They include construction workers in the construction industry, production workers in the manufacturing industry, and workers in the services sector who are not supervisors. About four in five workers are included in this group.

(As an aside, a subtly different question is whether productivity and wages are related, with wages thought of as a return to labor as a factor of production. For this, you'd want to look at all workers, not just typical workers. I won't focus on this point in this short book, but keep in mind that it's also an important consideration.)

You also need to decide how to adjust wages for inflation. Here, there are two leading contenders among economists and analysts: a consumer price index (CPI) research series, and the personal consumption expenditures (PCE) price index. (However, if you want to understand wages as compensation to a factor of production in the context of their relationship to productivity, you'd really want to use an output price deflator.)

The goal here is to capture the purchasing power of wages rather than the nominal value of wages. Nominal wages—that is, the amount listed on your paycheck—may be increasing, but if they are increasing at a rate slower than price inflation, the purchasing power of your wages is actually declining.

Take an example. Today, the nominal average wage of a typical (nonsupervisory) worker is about $24 per hour. In the fall of 1978, the nominal average wage was about one-fourth of that amount. But do today's workers enjoy four times the purchasing power as workers in the late 1970s? No. Because the prices workers must pay for goods and services have gone up.

It's more complicated than that, of course. Because as the prices of goods have risen, their quality has also improved. The price of an iPhone today is much higher than it was ten years ago. But iPhones today are also much more sophisticated—think of the improvements in camera quality alone—and higher-quality products. To compare the cost of an iPhone today with its cost ten years ago requires incorporating these quality adjustments so that you are really making an apples-to-apples comparison. And if you want to calculate how much prices have increased between the late 1970s and today, you have to account for the fact that there weren't any iPhones 40 years ago.

Both the CPI and PCE attempt to address these issues. There are numerous technical differences between the two, and each has its strengths and weaknesses. The CPI is specifically designed to capture the out-of-pocket expenditures made by consumers, whereas the PCE includes all expenditures made on behalf of consumers, including those made by third parties (for example, health insurance purchased for households by their employers or by the government). Depending on what you want to capture, each series may be more appropriate. The PCE has a broader scope than the CPI and does a better job capturing rural populations in addition to consumers who live in urban areas.

A major advantage of the PCE is its more realistic treatment of how consumers respond to price changes. The PCE is designed to account for consumer substitution between goods. If the price of strawberries goes up, for example, consumers might purchase fewer strawberries and more raspberries. By not accounting adequately for this type of substitution, the CPI overstates the price increases facing consumers. And by overstating those price increases, wages that are deflated by the CPI understate increases in purchasing power. (Indeed, the PCE likely overstates the actual rate of inflation as well, which implies that even it understates increases in real wage growth over time.)

In part because of its superior handling of consumer substitution between goods, the PCE is the preferred measure of the Federal Reserve[19] (although the Fed relies on a variety of price measures) and of the Congressional Budget Office. My conclusion is the same as theirs.

GROWTH OVER TIME

To figure out how much wages have grown for typical workers, you have to decide over which time period you want to look. Certainly, we want to compare the wages of today's workers to wages at some point in the past. But when?

The base-year selection is always somewhat arbitrary, of course, but we still need to pick one. I like to use July 1990, for a few reasons. Wage growth typically responds to the business cycle. To make comparisons of wage growth between two periods, then, it is important to try to find periods that are at a similar point in the business cycle. For example, comparing wage growth during a recession to wage growth during an expansion might bias the calculation to show stronger growth than may exist in the underlying trend. July 1990 was a business-cycle peak, making it a good month to compare to today's economy. (If anything, this date introduces a slight bias in favor of finding relatively weaker wage growth.)

Figure 7 is the same as the one that started this chapter. It looks as if wage growth can be broken into three periods: robust growth following the end of World War II, followed by a period of stagnant—or even declining—growth from the mid-1970s through the mid-1990s, followed again by a period of solid growth. So another reason to make comparisons to the summer of 1990 is that this was the business-cycle peak prior to the "structural break" that seems to have occurred in the mid-1990s.

FIGURE 7. AVERAGE REAL WAGE FOR PRODUCTION AND NONSUPERVISORY EMPLOYEES.

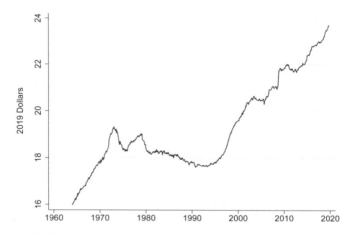

Average hourly earnings for production and nonsupervisory employees adjusted for inflation using the personal consumption expenditures price index.

Source: Bureau of Labor Statistics and Bureau of Economic Analysis data retrieved from FRED; author's calculations.

July 1990 is also roughly 30 years ago, which reflects the current narrative. You often hear that wages have been stagnant "for several decades," which many take to mean 30 years. Sometimes, you hear explicit references to 30 years—

for example, in Senator Hawley's speech mentioned in chapter 2.

But even when you don't hear this claim, when politicians and opinion leaders argue that wages have been stagnant for decades, people take that message as referring to *their* wages—that is, to the wages of people working today. Many of today's workers haven't been working for longer than 30 years, so that seems like pushing the outer limit of how far back you want to make this comparison. With respect to the political debate, going back further seems inadvisable.

Put it another way: Why should a politician, a commentator, or a worker care how much wages have grown since, say, 1973? That was 46 years ago. Very few of today's workers were in the labor force that long ago.

A lot of the debate about wage and income trends is focused on the proper way to adjust the data for inflation. This is why we spent a good amount of time on this topic in the previous section. Another argument for picking a comparison 30 years ago rather than, say, 50 years ago is that the closer you get to the present, the less it matters which inflation measure you choose. The measures increasingly agree the closer you get to the present day, as figure 8 shows.

Relatedly, it becomes much harder to make apples-to-apples comparisons between two periods the further into the past you go. Quality improvements are much harder to account for—a car in 1990 is much more similar to cars today than is a 1973 model—and fewer new products have been introduced. This is another argument against making comparisons between wages today and wages a half century ago.

I haven't mentioned 1973 several times by accident. That date is commonly used to make the argument that wages have stagnated. And as you can see in figure 8—which plots the wages of typical workers between 1973 and the present

FIGURE 8. AVERAGE REAL WAGE FOR PRODUCTION AND NONSUPERVISORY EMPLOYEES.

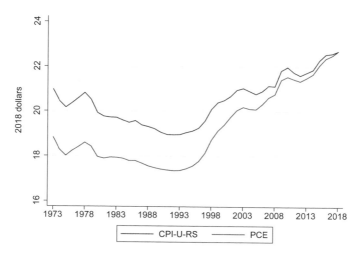

Average hourly earnings for production and nonsupervisory employees adjusted for inflation using the personal consumption expenditures price index (red line) and the consumer price index research series (blue line).

Source: Bureau of Labor Statistics and Bureau of Economic Analysis data retrieved from FRED; author's calculations.

using both the CPI research series (blue line) and the PCE (red line) price deflators—using the CPI shows that wages have grown by 5 percent. This is reasonably described as stagnant growth.

But as figure 8 shows, the conclusion of stagnation is largely a story of the poor performance of wage growth in the 1970s and 1980s. (It is also a story illustrating the extent to which the CPI overstates inflation. Wages deflated by the PCE increased by 21 percent between 1973 and 2018.[20])

Using either price deflator, just saying that wages have been stagnant since 1973 is an incomplete portrayal. Instead, it would be more accurate to say that wages were stagnant or falling during the 1970s and 1980s, and then in the 1990s began growing steadily.

Over the past three decades, wages for typical workers have grown by 20 percent using the CPI. And using the PCE—the better measure of inflation—finds a one-third increase in wages.

Have wages for typical workers grown more slowly over these decades than for, say, the top 1 percent? Of course. But a 20 percent increase in purchasing power is significant, to say nothing of a one-third increase. Steady annual gains have accumulated into a solid increase in inflation-adjusted wages. It's not spectacular growth, to be sure. But it is not reasonable to describe this growth as stagnant.

Here's the bottom line: Wages for typical workers have not stagnated for decades. Typical workers have not worked for several decades without a pay increase. A 34 percent increase in purchasing power over the last 30 years is not reasonably described as stagnant growth.

WHAT ABOUT MEDIAN WAGES AND THE BOTTOM HALF OF WORKERS?

Earlier we discussed two common measures of the "typical" worker. One is production and nonsupervisory workers, which we've focused on so far. Another is the median wage earner. Figure 9 shows this worker's wages over the past three decades.[21] They have increased by 24 percent. Though growth of one-quarter is less than the one-third increase in average wages for nonsupervisory employees, it still represents a significant increase in purchasing power. Median wages have not stagnated for the last several decades.

You might want to know about more than the growth of the typical worker's wages. What is happening to low-wage workers? The graph also shows the wages of the 10th, 20th, and 30th percentiles of the distribution.

Ninety percent of workers earn wages higher than the 10th percentile, and 10 percent earn lower wages. So these are low-wage workers. Likewise, 80 percent of workers earn more than the 20th percentile, and 20 percent earn less. The 30th percentile is calculated in the same way. Roughly speaking, these three percentiles capture low-wage workers and a good share of the working class.

FIGURE 9. AVERAGE REAL WAGE AT PERCENTILES OF THE WAGE DISTRIBUTION.

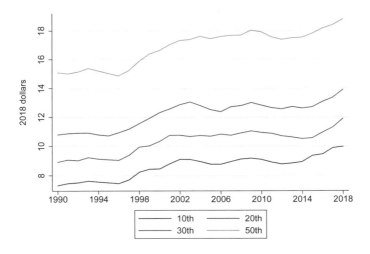

Source: Economic Policy Institute, State of Working America Data Library. Original data from the Bureau of Labor Statistics. Personal consumption expenditures price index data are from the Bureau of Economic Analysis. Note: EPI data were adjusted for inflation using the PCE by the author.

Although the median worker (or the "typical worker," in the language we've been using) earns more than the 10th, 20th, and 30th percentile workers, over the past 30 years those workers have enjoyed faster growth in wages. Wages at the 10th percentile have increased by 36 percent over this period. At the 20th percentile, wages have increased by 34 percent. And at the 30th percentile, they have increased by 29 percent.

We've seen that wages in the middle haven't been stagnant for decades. Instead, they've increased by a healthy amount. Wages for working-class and low-wage workers also haven't stagnated in recent decades.

PAY AND PRODUCTIVITY

The major reason that wages are growing is that workers are becoming more productive. The link between wages and productivity is strong.

This point, though, is also disputed. It's important because of the underlying implication: if productivity and pay are not strongly linked, then workers would not be enjoying the fruits of their labor. A fundamental moral proposition of the free enterprise system—that workers get their just deserts—would be failing.

This is ultimately an empirical question. To answer it, we first have to broaden our focus beyond wages. Though they are the most important component of total compensation, they are not all of it. For example, employer-provided health insurance is a major component of compensation.

We've been focusing on wages for a few reasons: They are the most salient component of compensation. They understandably play a large role in politics and in the public debate, so analyzing their behavior is important. We can be confident that workers and households do value other components of compensation, but it is difficult to assign a precise number to that value. This is not a problem for wages. And while all workers are paid wages (or salaries), not all receive the same benefits package.

But when studying the link between pay and productivity—when studying whether workers are receiving the fruits of their labor—benefits need to be included. Again, take health care. Its rising cost encourages firms to increase worker pay through health insurance benefits, rather than through wages and salaries.

The best paper I know of that directly addresses the link between pay and productivity is by economists Anna M. Stansbury and Lawrence H. Summers.[22] They study the pay of typical workers—measured both by the median wage and by wages of production and nonsupervisory workers—as well as the average wage of all workers. Stansbury and Summers deflate their compensation series using the CPI research series described above, rather than by an output price deflator. (As mentioned earlier, I would advise the latter, because economic theory argues that workers are paid the marginal product of the output they produce, not of the goods and services they consume.)

Stansbury and Summers have a straightforward empirical design. They calculate the three-year moving average of the change in real compensation and the three-year moving average of the change in labor productivity. They then correlate these smooth, short-run measures of compensation growth and productivity growth, holding constant effects from the business cycle. Their main results analyze the period from 1975 through 2015.

The economists find that a 1-percentage-point increase in productivity growth predicts a 0.73-percentage point increase in median compensation growth, a 0.53-percentage-point increase in compensation growth for nonsupervisory employees, and a 0.74-percentage-point increase in average compensation growth. In all three cases, their estimate is statistically significantly different from zero—that is, in a statistical sense, they can reject the hypothesis that there is no relationship between pay and productivity. For median and average compensation growth, they cannot reject the hypothesis that productivity growth maps to compensation growth one-to-one.

In other words, they find a very strong relationship between pay and productivity. "Our results suggest that productivity growth still matters substantially for middle-income Americans," Stansbury and Summers state.

"Overall, our central conclusion is as follows: the substantial variations in productivity growth that have taken place during recent decades have been associated with substantial changes in median and mean real compensation," they write. "This suggests that if productivity accelerates for reasons relating to technology or to policy, the likely impact will be increased pay growth for the typical worker."

This evidence supports the predictions of textbook microeconomics. And it contradicts the common narrative. The game isn't rigged for typical workers. Workers do enjoy the fruits of their labor.

INCOMES

Wages and total compensation are earned in the labor market. Studying income is also important—the flow of resources into a household that can be used for consumption and saving.

The nonpartisan Congressional Budget Office computes three income series. "Market income" is defined as labor income, employer-provided health insurance, business income, and capital income, along with retirement income for past services. "Income before taxes and transfers" is market income plus social insurance benefits, including Social Security payments, Medicare benefits, and payments from unemployment insurance, Social Security Disability Insurance, and workers' compensation. Finally, "income after taxes and transfers" is income before taxes and transfers plus means-tested transfers (e.g., Medicaid and Children's Health Insurance Program benefits, food stamp benefits, and Supplemental Security Income) minus federal taxes.

Each of these measures is instructive depending on the specific question you are trying to answer. For our purposes, looking at each of them is helpful. Median household market income increased by 21 percent between 1990 and 2016, the last year for which data are available. Like median wage growth, this is not spectacular and is less than household income for the top 1 percent. But it is not stagnant. (And if we had data for 2017 through the present, this growth would look even more impressive.)

The median household saw market income plus social insurance benefits increase by 28 percent from 1990 to 2016 (figure 10). And the most comprehensive measure of the income actually available to the median household to

FIGURE 10. CUMULATIVE GROWTH IN MEDIAN ANNUAL REAL HOUSEHOLD INCOME.

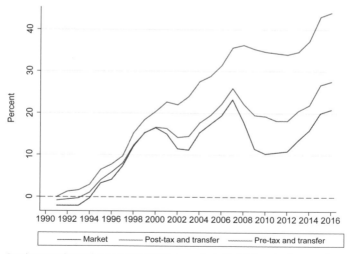

Cumulative growth in median annual household income, adjusted for inflation using the personal consumption expenditures price index and adjusted for household size.

Source: Congressional Budget Office; author's calculations.

spend and save—income after taxes and transfers—grew by 44 percent over this period.

Households in the bottom 20 percent of the income distribution are in a similar situation. Income after taxes and transfers increased by 66 percent over this period, 22 percentage points faster than for the median household. Income before taxes and transfers and market income both grew faster for these households than for those at the median (figure 11). The former increased by 34 percent, and the latter by 44 percent.[23]

FIGURE 11. CUMULATIVE GROWTH IN AVERAGE ANNUAL REAL HOUSEHOLD INCOME FOR THE FIRST INCOME QUINTILE.

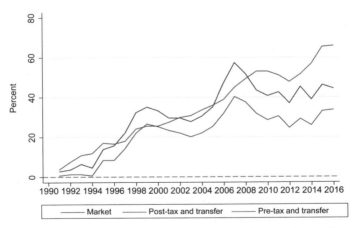

Cumulative growth in average annual household income, adjusted for inflation using the personal consumption expenditures price index.

Source: Congressional Budget Office; author's calculations.

For households in the middle and those nearer the bottom, income growth over the past three decades can't be reasonably described as stagnant. Instead, solid annual increases have accumulated to produce meaningful growth in the flow of resources generated by market activities that typical households can use for spending and saving.

WHAT ABOUT INEQUALITY?

Something interesting has been happening with income inequality—the gap between the rich and the poor—that is worth mentioning: it has stopped growing and might even be declining.

There are many ways to measure inequality, of course. You have to define income, decide on adjustments that need to be made to the data, and pick a statistic to measure inequality. Do you care about worker wages, household labor market earnings, or household income? How do you adjust for household size and inflation? Do you compute the size of the rich-poor gap by looking at the share of income held by the top 1 percent? Or by the ratio of the 90th percentile to the median? Or the ratio of the median to the 10th percentile?

The CBO uses the three household income measures described above and computes a "Gini coefficient" for each. This is a standard inequality statistic that summarizes income dispersion between households for the entire distribution of income.

The CBO found that income inequality between 1979 and 2006 increased by between 24 and 27 percent, depending on the definition of income. But things look very different between 2007 and 2016. Using market income, inequality has only grown by 2 percent. Using income after taxes and transfers, inequality has actually decreased by 7 percent (figure 12).

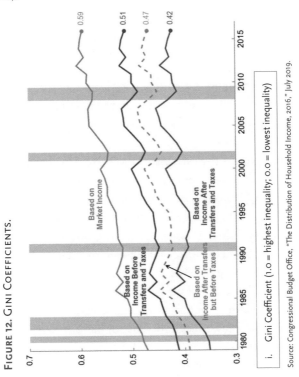

FIGURE 12. GINI COEFFICIENTS.

i.   Gini Coefficient (1.0 = highest inequality; 0.0 = lowest inequality)

Source: Congressional Budget Office, "The Distribution of Household Income, 2016," July 2019.

Looking at the usual weekly earnings of workers tells a similar story. Between 2007 and 2019, the ratio of the 90th percentile of weekly earnings to the 10th percentile—a more conceptually straightforward measure of the rich-poor gap—increased by only 1 percent.

So even if you believe that income inequality is one of the most serious challenges facing the United States, at least over the past decade or so, there seems to be a lot more heat than light.

Very recently, the public debate has become interested in wealth inequality, in addition to income inequality. I focus on inequality of income here for a few reasons. It has received the most attention during the post-Great Recession period—much more than wealth inequality. It is the more relevant measure for assessing disparities in the ability of different groups to consume and to save. It is hard to know what to make of changes in wealth inequality over time. To see why, consider this example: Expanded social insurance and safety net programs for lower- and middle-income households reduce the need for those households to accumulate assets. This exacerbates wealth inequality because it increases the gap in asset holdings between high-wealth and low-wealth households. Or consider that innovation can increase wealth inequality while reducing income inequality. In addition, wealth inequality is a difficult metric because it is much harder to measure wealth than to measure income. Many assets, like privately held businesses and pieces of art, aren't regularly traded in markets, and are unique. How much is the landscaping business owned by your neighbor worth? And what do you include in the definition of wealth? The value of savings accounts and stock portfolios, sure. But what about, say, the retirement pensions owed to public school teachers who are currently in their forties and fifties? What about human capital?

I'm more concerned about inequality between racial groups, men and women, and higher- and lower-skilled workers than I am about comparisons to the top 1 or top 0.1 percent. And I'm much more concerned about the absolute condition of the poor and the working class than I am about inequality. Later in the book I mention some policy solutions that would increase the earnings and incomes of these workers and households. This might reduce inequality as a side effect as well.

High Expectations Are Good

My goal here is not to be Panglossian or contrarian. Americans rightly have high expectations for wage and income growth. Gains over the past three decades have not been spectacular. We shouldn't be satisfied with them. One of the top goals for public policy should be faster wage and income growth, particularly for lower-wage workers and lower-income households.

And we shouldn't minimize the economic and psychological trauma of the Great Recession, which still lingers and whose damage will echo through the lives of millions of workers.

But despite these proper expectations and real challenges, the best analytical assessment concludes that wages for typical workers and income for typical households have not been stagnant for several decades. Wages and incomes also have not stagnated for the poor and the working class. And the tax and transfer system provides a significant increase in resources for those at the bottom.

The game is not rigged for all except those at the top. Workers do enjoy the fruits of their labor. As workers have grown more productive, those fruits have increased.

CHAPTER 7

Quality of Life Has Clearly Improved

><

THE ARGUMENT—and even the implication—that quality of life hasn't improved for typical households and individuals in decades shouldn't require the sort of analysis presented in the previous chapter to comprehensively refute. Indeed, the implication borders on the absurd.

Not long ago, color television was a luxury that most people could not afford. I happen to be writing the first draft of this chapter on a day that is 108 degrees Fahrenheit in Washington, so I am acutely aware of the benefits of air conditioning. It wasn't long ago that fewer than half of households had central air.[24] Staying in touch with friends and relatives who lived out of town used to be difficult because long-distance calls were so costly. I often actively enjoy my commute to Dupont Circle because my car is so comfortable and I have access to so much entertainment while driving. At the beginning of my career, commuting wasn't fun.

In 1980, 14 percent of women had a college degree. By 2018, the share of college-educated women had jumped to

35 percent. Men saw their college-degree attainment increase from 21 percent in 1980 to 35 percent in 2018.[25] In 1983, the median net worth for a family was approximately $52,000 (inflation-adjusted to 2016 dollars).[26] By 2016, median net worth had grown to $97,300.[27]

I don't want to take up too much space demonstrating the obvious in this short book, but here are some additional datums taken from two recent books, *The Rise and Fall of American Growth*, by the economist Robert Gordon, and *Enlightenment Now* by Stephen Pinker.:

- ▸ Improvements in heart attack survival rates from 1984 to 1998 yielded a one-year increase in life expectancy worth $70,000 for a $10,000 cost of improved medical technology.[28]

- ▸ According to Gordon, the mortality rate from cardio-vascular/renal disease has fallen from 500 people per 100,000 in 1970 to under 300 per 100,000 in 2007.[29] And by 2017, cardiovascular deaths had fallen to 165 per 100,000.[30]

- ▸ The development of antiretroviral therapy has improved quality of life for 1.2 million Americans with HIV and allowed them to have an "almost normal lifespan without experiencing serious illnesses related to their HIV infection."[31]

- ▸ Nearly 90 percent of households had computers, and nearly 80 percent had internet access by 2013. Nothing like personal computers nor the internet we know today existed 40 years ago.[32]

► From 1980 to 2013, air passenger fatalities fell from 100 per 100 billion passenger-miles to less than one fatality.[33]

► Between 2000 and 2012, the rate of diagnosis of dementia for Americans fell by one-quarter, and the average age of diagnosis rose from 80.7 to 82.4 years.[34]

► The average American worker with five years of experience receives 22 days of paid time off per year compared with 16 days in 1970.[35]

► The combination of a shorter workweek, more paid time off, and longer retirement means that the fraction of life taken up by work has fallen by a quarter since 1960.[36]

► Single and working mothers today spend more time with their children than stay-at-home married mothers did in 1965.[37]

► In 1974, it cost $1,442 (in 2011 dollars) to fly from New York to Los Angeles. By 2015, it cost less than $300.[38]

► Vehicle fatalities peaked in 1969 at 55,043. By 2012 the number of fatalities had fallen to 33,561, a decline of 39 percent. This decline occurred over a period in which vehicle miles traveled more than doubled.[39]

The common threads here are simple: instead of focusing

on pockets of problems, let's zoom out and focus on how some of the foundations of our quality of life—health, education, resources, day-to-day amenities, and experiences—have changed for the broad majority of Americans over the past several decades.

If you do that, the picture looks very good.

CHAPTER 8

"Hollowing Out" Won't Be the
End of the Story

⋝⋜

WHEN SHE ANNOUNCED her campaign for president, Senator Elizabeth Warren declared that she has "spent most of my life studying what happens to families like mine. Families caught in the squeeze. Families that go broke. What I found is that year after year, the path to economic security had gotten tougher and rockier." "Over the years," she asserted, "America's middle class has been deliberately hollowed out."[40] In the summer of 2019 Senator Josh Hawley asserted that the "elites" entered into an "alliance" with multinational corporations that resulted in, among other things, a "hollowed-out middle class."[41]

America's middle class has not been *deliberately* hollowed out in the sense that the senators argue. But the middle of the labor market has been hollowed out, and that has caused significant disruption.

You can see the hollowing out clearly in figure 13 from MIT economist David Autor.[42] The chart captures the change in the share of employment in nine broad occupation categories. The categories are ranked by the average wage of workers in that occupation. So workers in the "managers" occupation are the highest paid, and those in "health and personal services" occupations are lowest paid.

FIGURE 13. MIDDLE-SKILL, MIDDLE-WAGE JOBS HAVE BEEN SHRINKING AS A FRACTION OF TOTAL EMPLOYMENT.

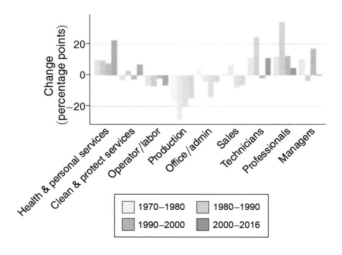

Source: David H. Autor, "Work of the Past, Work of the Future," Richard T. Ely Lecture, AEA Papers and Proceedings 109 (2019): 1–32.

Over the past four and a half decades, the share of total employment (as measured by total labor hours) working in technical, professional, and managerial occupations has increased considerably. The share of employment in low-wage health and personal services has increased as well. But employment in middle-skill, middle-wage occupations has been shrinking.

Autor finds that in 1970, total employment was evenly split across low-, middle-, and high-wage occupations, with 31 percent, 38 percent, and 30 percent of employment in each category, respectively. Employment in middle-wage, middle-skill occupations has since fallen significantly, to 23 percent of total employment.

In other words, the middle of the labor market hollowed out.

WHAT CAUSED THIS?

Think about what workers in those middle-skill, middle-wage occupations do. Many of their job tasks involve executing a series of steps with precision and accuracy. They often have to execute these steps repeatedly.

For example, a manufacturing worker on an assembly line has to repeat the same steps to put hubcaps on cars. Precision and accuracy are prized. A bookkeeper performs a similar function in carrying out basic accounting procedures. A bank teller must execute the same lists of steps in the same order for every cash withdrawal and deposit.

It happens that computers and robots are designed to execute procedures—to perform a list of steps. This, essentially, is what computers and robots do.

In a 2007 paper, economist William Nordhaus estimated that the cost of performing step-by-step computations with present-day computers is at least 1.7 trillion times cheaper than it was with manual computing.[43] And as the cost of computing has dropped, businesses have increasingly turned to technology to perform the types of rules-based procedures at which computers excel. So robots replaced manufacturing workers on assembly lines. ATMs replaced bank tellers. Software replaced bookkeepers.

Notice that the occupations at risk didn't include many of the lowest-skilled, least-paying occupations. The tasks in those jobs involve less step-by-step, precise execution than for jobs in the middle. For example, it turns out that it's quite difficult to write down a list of steps that would allow a robot to tell the difference between a pile of papers on a messy office floor that should not be thrown away at the end of the workday and trash that should be thrown away. A human custodian can readily tell the difference; a robot can't. And low-skill, low-wage workers in food preparation and service jobs need the ability to adapt to situations and interact with people. These tasks are also not amenable to being codified in step-by-step instructions.

Workers in high-skill, high-wage occupations often have to exercise sound managerial judgment, argue persuasively, be creative, and adapt to situations. As with the tasks required in low-wage occupations, it's hard to program computers and robots to do these well.

It is occupations in the middle—that paid better than those at the bottom because their tasks required precision and accuracy, but paid less than those at the top because workers in those occupations are relatively less skilled—that were hit hardest by automation, because their jobs were most amenable to being automated.

Those jobs included production and craft workers, machine operators and assemblers—exactly the types of jobs that have political salience today—the jobs that the president mistakenly argues were primarily affected by globalization (which was a factor, but not nearly as large a factor as automation), the jobs that didn't require a college degree but did offer a middle-class life.

The realities of a labor market that is hollowing out and, perhaps more significantly, offering diminished opportunities for entering the middle class have had a profound effect on society, culture, and politics. This longer-term, slower-burning, decades-long trend collided with the gut punch of the Great Recession, which contributed to the rise of populism and to the narrative that the American Dream is dead.

WILL THE MIDDLE MAKE A COMEBACK?

Fortunately, we have reason to believe that the middle might make a comeback.

In a recent paper, Georgetown University economist Harry Holzer draws a conceptual distinction between the "old middle" and the "new middle."[44] The old middle are what we think of as traditional middle-class jobs. They did not require a college degree, but in previous decades they paid enough to offer workers a middle-class life. These are the types of jobs—certain production, construction, and clerical occupations—that have been disappearing, and that have played a major role in the public debate these past few years, following the rise of populism.

I build on Holzer's insight and analysis here. Using data from the Bureau of Labor Statistics, I sort occupations based on the median wage earned by workers in that occupation. I then look at the middle-wage occupations. Specifically, I examine the middle third of occupations by pay—the occupations for which one-third of all occupations pay more and one-third pay less. I do this for every year from 2000 to 2018, and I look at how the jobs that are included in the middle third change over time. I divide jobs into two groups: the old middle and the new middle.

I assign three broad occupational categories to the old middle: production occupations, construction and extraction occupations, and clerical occupations. The specific jobs in those broad occupation categories include assemblers (of aircraft, electrical and electronic equipment, engines and other machines), metal fabricators and fitters, meat packers, poultry and fish cutters and trimmers, machine setters, furnace operators, metal pourers and casters, tool and die makers, brick masons, welders, carpenters, construction laborers, telephone operators, payroll and timekeeping clerks, file clerks, typists, and secretaries and administrative assistants.

Jobs that are not in the old middle but that are still in the middle one-third of the occupation-wage distribution I classify as belonging to a new middle. These jobs are found in several broad occupational categories: health-care support occupations, transportation, education and training, and personal care and service, to name a few.

Figure 14 shows that jobs in the old middle are indeed declining as a share of overall employment. Overall, middle-

FIGURE 14. SHARE OF EMPLOYMENT IN MIDDLE-INCOME OCCUPATIONS.

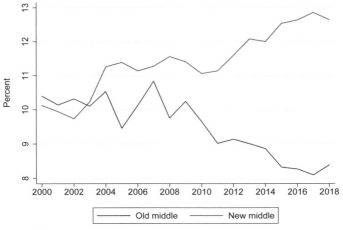

See text for description.

Source: Bureau of Labor Statistics; author's calculations.

wage production, construction, and clerical jobs—the old middle, represented by the blue line—have fallen from around 10 percent of total employment to 8 percent of total employment over the past two decades.

Production jobs that fell in the middle third of the occupation-wage distribution constituted about 3 percent of total employment in the year 2000. By 2018, that had fallen by one-third, to 2 percent. Middle-wage clerical jobs made up 6 percent of total employment in 2000 but now only make up 4 percent.

But as that has happened, middle-wage jobs that are not in what we think of as traditional middle-wage occupational categories have seen considerable growth. Over the past two decades, the share of total employment in new middle jobs— that is, in middle-wage jobs that are not in the traditional middle-class occupational categories, and represented by the red line—increased by 25 percent, from around 10 percent to 12.5 percent.

Over the past half-decade, the fastest-growing jobs in the new middle include sales representatives, truck drivers, managers of personal service workers, heating and air conditioning mechanics and installers, computer support specialists, self-enrichment education teachers, event planners, health technologists and technicians, massage therapists, social workers, marriage and family counselors, audiovisual technicians, paralegals, health-care social workers, chefs and head cooks, and food service managers.

These jobs probably require a little more education, skills, and experience than jobs in the old middle. They require more situational adaptability, social intelligence, customer service and interpersonal interaction, low-end managerial skills, and administrative, technical, and communication skills.

So, yes, populists on the left and right are correct that traditional middle-class jobs are shrinking as a share of total employment. These middle-class jobs do represent a hollowing out of the middle. But in recent decades, a new middle is emerging.

DYNAMISM

Changes in the types of jobs represented in the middle of the labor market is a reality of economic dynamism. Yes, dynamism has negative effects and accrues to the detriment of some workers. Many new middle jobs will have aspects that are less desirable than the jobs they replaced. But dynamism has an upside as well. It creates new opportunities. Creative destruction destroys—but it also creates.

Political and opinion leaders have done an excellent job in recent years of focusing on the negative effects of dynamism, with scant mention of its benefits. We have heard a lot about manufacturing jobs taking a hit. We have heard very little about new opportunities for high-end services and health-care technicians.

We have also heard little about this important finding: Recall that David Autor, the economist, calculated that over the four-and-a-half decades since 1970, middle-skill employment fell from about 38 percent to 23 percent of total employment. But this fall in the middle was offset by a rise in employment at the top. Employment in high-skill occupations grew from about 30 percent to 46 percent. At the same time, low-skill employment did not increase. On the whole, the hollowing out of the middle is a story of middle-skill employment being replaced by high-skill employment.

Figure 15 may be more intuitive. Using data from the U.S. Census Bureau,[45] I graph the share of households with total inflation-adjusted incomes of $35,000 or less, the share with incomes between $35,000 and $100,000, and the share with incomes higher than $100,000. Data in the graph begin in 1967 and go through 2018.

These cutoff points are arbitrary, but they are designed to capture the evolution of the middle class. The share of households in the middle has fallen from 54 percent to 42 percent. Where did they go? The share of low-income households (those earning less than $35,000) has fallen as well over this period, from 36 percent in 1967 to 28 percent in 2018. But the share of households earning over $100,000 has tripled, rising from 10 percent to 30 percent.

The picture is not as rosy as this makes it seem. There are pockets of problems—in this case, for workers with relatively little education, whose experience of the middle hol-

FIGURE 15. SHARE OF HOUSEHOLDS BY INCOME GROUP.

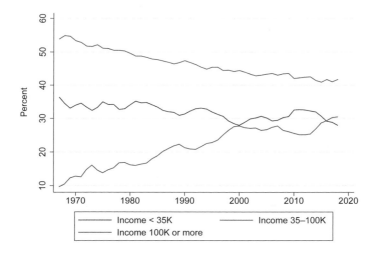

Share of households in each income group. Income statistics are taken from the Census Bureau's report, "Income and Poverty in the United States: 2018." Income is defined as money income received before taxes, and not including noncash government benefits.

Source: Census Bureau; author's calculations.

lowing out was not typical in that it found some who were in middle-class jobs falling into lower-skilled, lower-paid jobs. But a theme of this book applies: we should not confuse pockets of serious problems with the norm.

We also have heard very little about the holistic effects of these changes. Take ATMs and bank tellers. I wrote above that ATMs replaced tellers. But that isn't the whole story. Retail bank branches are not simply automated teller machines. Human beings work in those branches. But the tasks those workers perform in their jobs have changed. Cash handling is less important—the ATMs can do that. Instead, interpersonal and problem-solving skills have become more important. Relationship management is a skill in demand. The branches still need workers—just to do different things.

This is the broader lesson: Certain job tasks can be automated. But most jobs represent a bundle of tasks, some of which are quite difficult to automate. As technology advances and becomes cheaper, situational adaptability, interpersonal interaction, judgment and common sense, and communications skills will become more valuable, because they complement technological change rather than substitute for it. And jobs will require more tasks using these skills.

It makes sense that as traditional middle-class jobs—the old middle—become a smaller share of the economy, a new middle has arisen. Labor-saving technology in some occupations creates a pool of available workers, and businesses have an incentive to find ways to use those workers. Again, the skills they are looking for and the tasks they need accomplished can be different. But the incentive to put the talents and efforts of America's labor force to work is a powerful one to which businesses have responded.

The populist response to technological change is wrong. We shouldn't bemoan it. We shouldn't attempt to turn back the clock. We shouldn't wish to revive shrinking occupations and reverse the productivity gains—and increases in quality of life—made possible by technological change.

Instead, we should be working to ensure that the institutions that impart worker skills—schools, public programs, private businesses—are up to the challenge of equipping workers with what they need to flourish in the 21st-century economy. Workers themselves need to be willing to adapt to change and to do what is necessary, though often very difficult, to flourish in a dynamic economy.

And we should remember that economic dynamism is much more a blessing than it is a curse.

CHAPTER 9

America Is an Upwardly Mobile Society

— ≥≤ —

C ENTRAL TO the American Dream is the idea of economic mobility. We started on that in a previous chapter on wage and income growth. But growing wages and incomes for typical workers tells a subtly different story than whether workers are economically mobile, and whether America on the whole is characterized by economic mobility. The issue here is whether America has become a "class society," or whether Horatio Alger is still alive and well.

I conclude the latter. Specifically:

▸ The rags-to-riches concept of the American Dream is present in the data, with about seven Americans out of every 100 who were raised in the bottom 20 percent of the income distribution reaching the top 20 percent as adults.

▸ Around three-quarters of Americans have higher (inflation-adjusted) family incomes than did their parents.

▸ Eighty-six percent of Americans raised in the bottom 20 percent have higher family incomes than did their parents. We should be most concerned about upward mobility for the lowest-income Americans, and by this measure the vast majority have such mobility.

▶ For adults raised in the working class (the second quintile of the income distribution), about three-quarters have higher income than their parents. This group is particularly important given their political salience to populists on the left and right, including the president and those Democrats running to succeed him.

▶ The narrative that income mobility has declined for birth cohorts since the 1940s is true, but also exaggerated.

▶ When considering labor market earnings rather than income, most American men (around 59 percent) earn more than their fathers earned.

▶ About eight in ten sons raised in the bottom 20 percent go on to out-earn their fathers. This statistic demonstrates significant earnings mobility from the bottom.

▶ Close to three-quarters of sons raised in the working class have gone on to earn more than their fathers.

INCOME RANK COMPARISONS

A common way to assess the degree to which a society is economically mobile is to compare income rank across generations.

To unpack this, we must first define "income rank." Imagine there are only 100 families in the economy. Rank them from 1 to 100, such that the highest-income family is ranked number 1 and the lowest-income family is ranked number 100. Now sort these families into five equally sized groups, called "quintiles." Each quintile will have 20 families, with families ranked 1 through 20 in the top quintile, families ranked 21 through 40 in the second quintile, and so on. You now have a "quintile rank" for each family. That is, for every family, you know whether they are in the first (bottom), second, third (middle), fourth, or fifth (top) quintile based on their income—or, more precisely, based on their income rank.

Of course, you can do the same thing for more than 100 families. But the exercise remains the same: rank the families by income and assign each family to one of five equally sized quintile groups.

Now imagine that there are two generations: "parents" and "children." Calculate a quintile rank for each family in the "parents" generation when the parents are adults, and for each family in the "children" generation when the children are adults. Because we are following families across generations, we know the income rank of the family in which a child was raised when that child was young—that is, the "parents" income rank—and we know the income rank of the family in which the child is an adult, heading the household.

If children raised in the bottom quintile—that is, in the bottom 20 percent—remain in the bottom quintile as adults, we might argue that there is excessive "stickiness" in income across generations. We might question our understanding of America as an upwardly mobile society. We might argue that America has become a class society. On the other hand, if children raised in the bottom quintile achieve a higher income rank as adults, then we might argue the opposite.

Data and Measurement

To study mobility, I analyze data from the Panel Study of Income Dynamics (PSID), a data set that has followed families from 1968 to the present. The PSID records information about a household and then follows the children from that household when they grow up and start families of their own. It contains a wealth of information about families across generations and allows the comparison of members of different generations at the same point in their life cycles.

It might be tempting to look at someone's family income rank today and compare it to her family's income rank for a year when she was a child. The problem with that comparison is that income fluctuates from year to year. In any given year, a lawyer might win a big case, or a retail salesperson might pick up a lot of overtime, or a factory worker might be on temporary layoff. If you want to know whether people who are born at the top stay at the top, you wouldn't want your analysis driven by these transitory, year-to-year fluctuations in income. Instead, you want to look at the underlying trend in income around which these fluctuations occur. You want to look at the steadier, "structural" component of income—what economists refer to as "permanent income."

A second, related issue is that income changes with a person's life cycle. You wouldn't want to compare someone's income at age 45 with another person's income at age 25 and draw any conclusions about which person has a higher "permanent income," because as a general matter, people earn more in their 40s than they do in their 20s. For a starker example, if you want to know whether John earns more than his father, you wouldn't want to compare their income today if John's father is retired. Instead, you'd want to compare their incomes at the same age, or in the same point in their life cycles.

A third issue deals with adjustments to income. Income is important because it is the flow of resources from which a household can consume (or save). But because, for any given standard of living, adding, say, a fourth person to a household of three requires fewer additional resources than adding a second person to a household of one, household size—which has been falling on average over time—needs to be taken into account when comparing income between households. In addition, in order to make apples-to-apples comparisons across time, income needs to be adjusted for inflation. Reflecting these considerations, the measure of family income used here includes income from labor market earnings, interest, dividends, and cash transfers (including, for example, Social Security) of family members.

RELATIVE MOBILITY FOR AMERICAN ADULTS

Using the PSID data, I gather people who are in their 40s in recent years (2013–2017). To compute a measure of their permanent income, I take the average of their annual income across the years when they are in their 40s. I adjust income for household size following a standard method and adjust for inflation using the PCE. I then compute an income quintile rank for these current 40-somethings. [46]

I want to know whether their rank is the same as the rank of the family in which they grew up. I then follow the same procedure for their parents. Specifically, I identify the household in which they grew up and compute size-adjusted family income for the years in which the head of their childhood household was in his or her 40s. I average income across these years in order to mitigate the influence of transitory fluctuations. Then I compute the income quintile rank for these households.

Figure 16 summarizes the results. Each of the five vertical bars captures the income quintile in which today's adults were raised—that is, their parents' quintile. The color-coded segments within each vertical bar show where today's adults ended up. For example, 19.2 percent of today's 40-somethings

FIGURE 16. FAMILY INCOME MOBILITY.

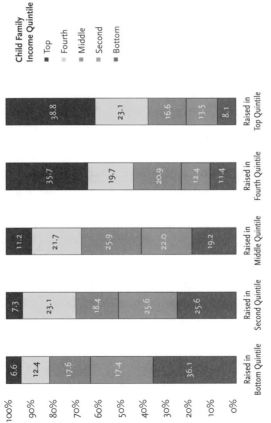

See text for description.

Source: Panel Study of Income Dynamics; author's calculations.

raised in the middle quintile as children ended up in the bottom quintile as adults. Twenty-two percent of today's adults raised in the middle quintile ended up in the second quintile. And around 11 percent of adults raised in the middle quintile have made it to the top 20 percent.

Is Income Rank "Sticky"?

If you are born at the top, will you stay at the top as an adult? If you are born at the bottom, can you make it to the top when you become an adult? How "sticky" is income rank within the same family across generations?

About 36 percent of children raised in the bottom 20 percent—in the bottom income quintile—remain there as adults, and about 39 percent of children raised in the top quintile are themselves in the top when they are in their 40s (figure 17).

I am paid to have strong opinions about these sorts of statistics, but I honestly don't know what to make of them. On the one hand, arguing that one-third of children raised in the bottom remain there when they reach their prime earning years makes America seem like a class society. On the other hand, arguing that two-thirds of children raised in the bottom escape that position as adults makes America seem quite upwardly mobile.

The same issue presents itself with stickiness at the top. Thirty-nine percent of children born there stay there. That sounds sticky. But what if, instead, I characterized the data

FIGURE 17. FAMILY INCOME STICKINESS.

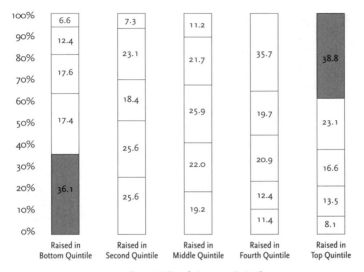

Parents' Family Income Quintile

See text for description.

Source: Panel Study of Income Dynamics; author's calculations.

as saying that well over half of children raised at the top do not remain at the top as adults?

RAGS TO RICHES

One common conceptualization of living the American Dream is the *possibility*—not the *certainty*—of going from rags to riches. That is to say, the American Dream is alive and well if it is possible to be born poor and to end up rich.

FIGURE 18. RAGS TO RICHES.

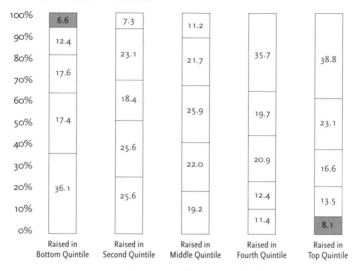

Parents' Family Income Quintile

See text for description.

Source: Panel Study of Income Dynamics; author's calculations.

Of course, that this is discussed as a possibility implies that it does not have to happen to everyone, or even happen often, for the Dream to be in good health. But it has to happen often enough not to be a complete shock when we see it.

Figure 18 presents data on both rags to riches and riches to rags. It shows that around 7 percent of children raised in the bottom 20 percent make it to the top as adults. (And around 8 percent of children raised at the top end up at the bottom.)

On this measure, the American Dream seems to be a reality.

RAGS TO COMFORT

But rags to riches doesn't apply to the broad swath of American society. What about rags to comfort? Or, more generally, movement upward, toward the top?

Figure 19 shows that around 30 percent of children raised in the bottom 20 percent end up in either the third or fourth

FIGURE 19. RAGS TO COMFORT.

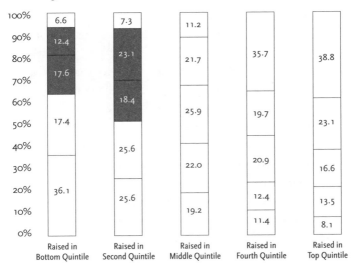

Parents' Family Income Quintile

See text for description. Source: Panel Study of Income Dynamics; author's calculations.

quintiles as adults. They don't reach the top 20 percent, but they do end up comfortably in the middle, achieving a higher income rank than their parents. Similarly, about 42 percent of children raised in the second quintile move up one or two quintiles as adults.

Is Relative Mobility the Best Mobility Concept to Use?

I mentioned earlier that I have a hard time interpreting these relative, or rank-based, mobility statistics. It is very difficult to know the "right amount" of relative mobility, or the amount of relative mobility that corresponds to a just society, or to a society that meets the demands of the American Dream.

It would of course be a problem if there were no relative mobility in American society—if every child grew up to have the same income rank as his parents, if every child raised in the top 20 percent stayed in the top 20 percent, and if every child raised in the bottom 20 percent remained there as well. This society would clearly be immobile and would clearly not fit with America's conception of itself.

At the same time, we wouldn't want a society with mathematically perfect relative mobility. We wouldn't want a child raised in the top 20 percent to have a one-in-five chance of being in the top 20 percent as an adult, and a one-in-five chance of being in the bottom 20 percent. For one reason, we would expect parental investments in their children to matter, so a situation of perfect mobility would correspond to a zero return on parental investment, or no relationship between investment and income. Either situation seems problematic.

So we want something between no mobility and perfect mobility. How much? Many argue that we currently have too little mobility. But how much more mobile should we be? How would we know?

Another challenge with interpreting rank-based mobility statistics is that they don't necessarily correlate with improvements in living standards. The bottom half of the income distribution could all see their living standards decline at the same time that it became more likely for children raised in the bottom to rise to the top. Most Americans would feel like the United States had stepped further away from the American Dream in this scenario, even though relative mobility would have improved.

A final challenge I have with relative mobility: I find it difficult to support on moral grounds. I am of course eager for more children raised in the bottom to rise to the top. But because relative mobility is rank-based, for every person who moves up the ladder, someone else has to move down. If you are cheering for more upward mobility, you are necessarily also cheering for downward mobility. I find it something of a struggle to cheer enthusiastically for downward mobility.

Absolute Mobility

In contrast to relative mobility, absolute mobility is easier to interpret and, for me at least, to support. It asks a simple question: Are you doing better during, say, your 40s than your parents were doing during their 40s? This comparison is irrespective of income rank. Instead, if people are doing better as adults than in the circumstances in which they were raised, we conclude that America is upwardly mobile. If they aren't, we conclude it isn't.

It's easy to know how much absolute mobility we want in America: more! Absolute mobility corresponds directly with improving standards of living. And it is easy to support increasing absolute mobility on moral grounds. Everyone can do better under this concept of mobility. Looking at mobility through this lens, no one has to do worse for you to do better.

Using the same data and definitions as before, I compute absolute mobility statistics. Overall, I find that around 73 percent of Americans in their 40s have higher incomes than did their parents. (figure 20)

Among children raised in the bottom 20 percent, 86 percent have gone on to enjoy higher incomes than their parents. That is, 86 percent of today's 40-somethings who were raised in the bottom 20 percent have higher incomes than their parents did when their parents were in their 40s. This is particularly important since upward mobility from the

FIGURE 20. SHARE OF ADULT CHILDREN WITH HIGHER TOTAL FAMILY INCOMES THAN THEIR PARENTS.

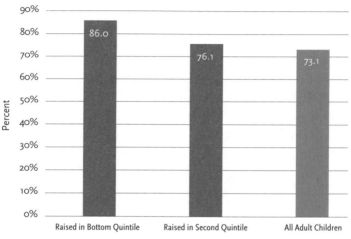

Parents' Total Family Income Quintile

See text for description. Source: Panel Study of Income Dynamics; author's calculations.

bottom of the income distribution is what we should care about most.

For adults who were raised in the second quintile, about 76 percent enjoy a higher income than their parents. This is important because this quintile represents many in the working class, a group that has received considerable attention from populists in both political parties, including President Trump and several Democratic presidential candidates running in the 2020 primary season.

In the middle quintile (not shown in figure 20), upward absolute income mobility measures around 77 percent. In the fourth quintile, it's also around 74 percent. And about 53 percent of 40-somethings today in the top 20 percent have a higher income than their parents did when their parents were in their 40s.

This analysis suggests that America is clearly an upwardly mobile society. The common experience is for children to have higher incomes than their parents. This is particularly true of children raised in the bottom 20 percent, and, really, for those raised outside the top 20 percent.

How Much More?

Adults today typically earn a good deal more than their parents. In other words, America isn't upwardly mobile by just a few cents.

I should first caution you not to read too much into the exact numbers because the sample size of the PSID is not especially large. With that in mind, after all the sample restrictions necessary for this analysis have been imposed, the median income of a 40-something today is about $54,000. The median income of the family in which today's 40-somethings were raised when the head of that household was in his or her 40s was about $35,000. So around 73 percent of today's 40-somethings have a higher household income than their parents did when their parents were in their 40s—and it is higher by about $19,000.[47]

Adults who were raised in the bottom quintile have a family income about 2.5 times as large as their parents did when their parents were in their 40s. And across all quintiles, adults today have higher family incomes than did their parents.

Is the American Dream in decline?

A few years ago, an academic paper by a distinguished team of scholars—Raj Chetty, David Grusky, Maximilian Hell, Nathaniel Hendren, Robert Manduca, and Jimmy Narang—found that only 50 percent of people born in the early 1980s went on to have higher incomes than their parents when they reached age 30, down from more than 90 percent for children born in the early 1940s (figure 21).[48]

This paper received an enormous amount of attention from the media, prompting headlines about the death of the American Dream. The authors themselves assert in the paper's title that the Dream is fading.

There is no doubt about this paper's importance to our understanding of economic mobility. And a lead author on the paper, Harvard professor Raj Chetty, is one of the most important economists in the world today. He will certainly deserve the Nobel Prize he is quite likely to receive, due in large part to his pathbreaking work studying economic opportunity in America.

Despite this paper's importance, reaction to it has been overstated, both with respect to the finding that only half

FIGURE 21. PERCENTAGE OF CHILDREN EARNING MORE THAN THEIR PARENTS, BY YEAR OF BIRTH.

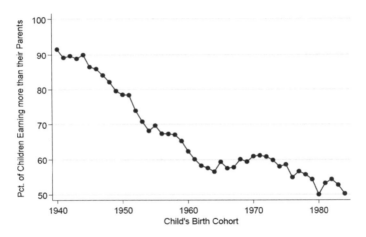

Source: Raj Chetty, David Grusky, Maximilian Hell, Nathaniel Hendren, Robert Manduca, and Jimmy Narang, "The Fading American Dream: Trends in Absolute Income Mobility Since 1940," *Science*, vol. 356, no. 6336, 2017.

of adults today will out-earn their parents and to the downward trend the researchers presented.

The paper itself reports a better estimate of the level of absolute mobility for people born in the early 1980s than the headline number of 50 percent. If you read deep into the paper, you will find that adjusting income for household size bumps the 50 percent estimate up to 60 percent. It is standard practice in the economics literature to adjust income for household size, and I would have chosen 60 percent, rather than 50 percent, as the headline number.

Chetty and his coauthors use the CPI research series discussed in a previous chapter to adjust incomes for inflation. Social scientist Scott Winship estimates that using the PCE to adjust income for inflation would increase the Chetty et al. estimate from 60 percent (taking into account the household-size adjustment) to 67 percent.[49]

So, with these two tweaks—adjusting for household size, and using what I would argue is the superior measure of inflation—the headline changes from "half of Americans have lower incomes than their parents" to "one-third of Americans have lower incomes than their parents." That's quite a difference. It's also much closer to my own estimate of around one-quarter.

As to the trend, Chetty's work has convinced me that economic mobility was higher for people born in the 1940s than for those born in more recent decades—that is, that mobility has been declining. But a decline from 90 percent to two-thirds or three-quarters is much less troubling than a decline to one-half.

And is it really a surprise that children born in or shortly after the Great Depression era go on to earn more than their parents in overwhelming numbers? Indeed, it is more surprising that one in ten of these children *did not* go on to earn more than their parents than it is that nine in ten did.

This speculation goes beyond Chetty's detailed data set, but it seems at least equally plausible to me that absolute income mobility was artificially high for people born in the decades after the 1930s, and that what Chetty and his colleagues find for the last few decades of birth cohorts represents something closer to the norm, rather than a major decline from the norm.

EARNINGS

Throughout this chapter, we have been studying income mobility. But intergenerational mobility of earnings—a subset of income—is also important to consider. Whether Americans today earn more in the labor market than their parents did is critical if you believe that earnings are a uniquely important source of income to a sense of contribution and personal dignity.

To examine this, I compare the earnings of fathers and sons. It is common not to include females in this type of analysis, because their patterns of labor supply are less steady than for men, and because the effects of the significant increase in female labor force participation over this time period would be difficult to separate from earnings mobility. I also do not size-adjust these comparisons, as they are one to one. Finally, the earnings number includes wages, salaries, commissions, tips, bonuses, and the like—earnings from the labor market. Other than those items, the analysis here is the same as for income.

The patterns of relative, rank-based mobility for father-son earnings are similar to family income. About one-third of sons raised in the bottom quintile remain there as adults, and around one-third of sons raised in the top 20 percent remain when they are in their 40s. As with income mobility, whether this is excessively sticky is a matter of interpretation.

About 12 percent of sons raised in the bottom quintile are top-quintile earners as adults, showing that the rags-to-riches version of the American Dream is present in earnings as well as income. And well over half of sons who were raised in the bottom two quintiles end up in a higher quintile that is not the top quintile as adults, so there is considerable rags-to-comfort at work in earnings.

Six in ten (or around 59 percent) of American men in their 40s earn more than their fathers earned when their fathers were in their 40s. So most men out-earn their fathers, though there is less mobility when measured with earnings than income (figure 22). About 79 percent of sons raised in the bottom 20 percent go on to outearn their fathers. This statistic shows significant earnings mobility from the bottom, which is arguably what we should care about most.

Close to three-quarters of sons raised in the second quintile—the 21st through 40th percentiles of the earnings distribution, which includes many in the working class—have gone on to earn more than their fathers.

Around six in ten sons raised in the middle outearned their fathers, and fewer than half of sons raised in the top 40 percent went on to do so. This highlights that sons raised

FIGURE 22. SHARE OF ADULT MEN WITH HIGHER LABOR INCOME THAN THEIR FATHERS.

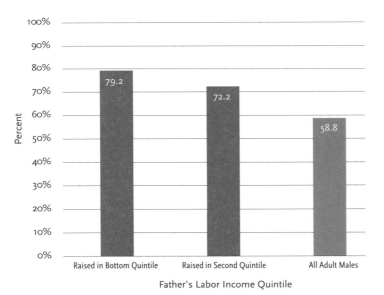

See text for description.

Source: Panel Study of Income Dynamics; author's calculations.

in the bottom are more upwardly mobile than those raised closer to the top.

How much more? As with income, a word of caution about the sample size here is needed. Having said that, the median adult son in this sample is in his 40s during the 2013–2017 period, and earns about $62,000, or about $6,000 more than his father earned when his father was in his 40s. In other words, the median adult son earns around 11 percent more than did his father when his father was the same age.[50]

This central tendency is driven in part by the fact that adult sons raised in the top 40 percent of the parent earnings distribution went on to earn less than their fathers. Focusing on the bottom of the parent earnings distribution—which is what we should care about most—finds significant earnings gains across these generations. Sons raised in the bottom 20 percent went on to earn around 1.6 times as much as their fathers. Sons raised in the second quintile—roughly, the working class—earned 30 percent more as adults than their fathers earned.

Even still, these results highlight the need for policies to increase earnings mobility, with the goal that more sons go on to out-earn their fathers, including those raised nearer the top.

Discussion

Wrapping your arms fully around economic mobility is hard, and this chapter is not intended to be a comprehensive summary. We've looked at mobility of income and earnings, but you might also be interested in mobility of wealth, education, and occupation. We've looked at intergenerational mobility, but you might also be interested in mobility within a generation.

You might also be interested in different groups of Americans. The point of this short book is to present the broad picture, so I haven't offered mobility results for different races. While African Americans were included in this analysis, as a group they are noticeably less mobile than white Americans. This is troubling.

Americans should not be complacent. We should hope for and work toward a future where incomes grow more rapidly within the same family across generations, where more children go on to outearn their parents, and by wider margins. Americans rightly have high expectations.

Could there be more upward mobility in America? Yes. But if you have to pick between characterizing America as upwardly mobile or upwardly immobile—if you have to pick between the American Dream of upward mobility being alive or dead, between America being a class society or not—the right choice in that binary is upwardly mobile. America is upwardly mobile. America is not a class society, where no intergenerational progress takes place. The American Dream is not dead.

Of course, what we care about most is whether today's young people will be upwardly mobile, not whether today's 40-year-olds did better than their parents. We should pursue that goal aggressively, acting as if the American Dream is under threat, even if we believe it's not.

CHAPTER 10
Advancing the Dream

≥≤

THE LAST chapter closed on a critical point: We should aggressively advance the American Dream.

The economy is delivering for workers today. Over the past three decades, wages and incomes have grown for typical workers and for low-income workers. Workers do enjoy the fruits of their labor. Quality of life has improved. Economic dynamism has created change in the middle of the labor market, seeing employment reductions in some occupations but growth in others, and seeing employment losses in middle-skill jobs mostly replaced by higher-skill jobs. Today's adults typically experienced significant upward mobility relative to their parents—particularly those raised in the bottom 20 percent and in the working class. The game isn't rigged for everyone except those at the top.

Whether the Dream is alive and well today certainly matters. Arguably, it matters more whether it will continue to be alive and well over the coming decades. Policymakers should not take this analysis as an excuse for complacency. Public policy should aggressively advance the American Dream.

Our policies should tackle the serious pockets of problems that are properly in the headlines, including opioid addiction, deaths of despair, and the troubling increase in suicides. Public policy should do what it can to increase social capital and strengthen institutions, associational life, and family life. It should address workers who are not faring as well as typical workers—men without a high school education, for example. It should be concerned about relatively lower rates of mobility among the African American community. And more.

Policymakers should also work to strengthen the Dream as the solid majority of Americans will experience it. Managing the effects of advancing technology and globalization, increasing workforce participation rates, addressing an inadequate educational system, reenergizing the workforce, increasing dynamism, accelerating productivity growth—we have much to do.

Populism

A major threat to the American Dream is the rising tide of populism on both the political left and right.

Motivated by the incorrect belief that the system is rigged in favor of "the elites," populists on the left are advocating extreme policies: $15 minimum wages, "Medicare for All," free college tuition, forgiving student loan debt, special and punitive tax rules for the richest U.S. households. Proliferating entitlement programs, harmful regulation, and punishing the rich are not in the long-term interest of American workers and families.

Populism on the political right exists as more than just policy proposals, because the Republican Party has put a populist in the Oval Office. The Trump administration is damaging the post–World War II liberal international order, which has supported American prosperity for decades. President Trump has rejected the GOP's traditional emphasis on the need to reduce projected future spending on Medicare and Social Security. This emphasis has been correct both to protect our commitment to the elderly by placing these programs on secure footing and to free up political space for other priorities—including priorities that would advance the American Dream.

The president, many in the GOP, and many conservatives routinely demonize immigrants. A national conversation about immigration policy and border security is necessary; reasonable people of goodwill can disagree about the appropriate number of green cards to issue each year and the characteristics of the immigrant pool to which they are issued. But stoking racial animosity is deeply harmful. It threatens the American Dream in myriad ways, the way termites threaten the integrity of a house—by rotting its very core.

The president's populist protectionism has proven to be a major risk to the stability of the global economy, significantly increasing the likelihood of recession. Of course, the working class he rhetorically champions would be among the hardest hit by any recession to which his protectionist policies contribute. Following the populists' lead, many conservative policy analysts and writers are warming to protectionism as well.

Many on the right are also downplaying the importance of economic growth, which is to say that they are downplaying improvements in the well-being of American workers and families over the longer term. Some on the political right are even warming to industrial policy.

Both the populist left and right are turning inward—anxious about the future, closed to the world, attempting to return to an imagined past, intoxicated with nostalgia or with the concept of an unattainable utopian future. Both are retreating from the importance of personal responsibility, embracing a narrative of victimhood, and treating those with whom they disagree as enemies to be defeated rather than as fellow citizens with whom to compromise. Americans are bombarded with this message:

Your economic situation is not your responsibility. It happened to you, was caused by the elites, and there is nothing you can do to change it. You have no agency. Immigrants are to blame. The wealthy are to blame. The game is rigged. Free trade is good for the elites, but not for you. Economic growth is good for the elites, but not for you. The game is zero-sum, us versus them, and it's time to fight back.

MESSAGES MATTER

In addition to the threat populist policies pose to the American Dream, the populist narrative of grievance and message of victimhood is damaging.

For starters, it is analytically incorrect. As we've discussed, in the U.S. economy, workers enjoy the fruits of their labor. People aren't helpless victims; they have agency, and their effort has a direct impact on their success.

The common experience over the past several decades has been that jobs are readily available for those who want them, and for quality of life to improve. The populist argument that typical workers have been at a standstill for decades—victims of an elite that has "rigged the system" against them to help itself, or of immigrants—is incorrect.

And because it is incorrect, this message—espoused by some of our most prominent and important elected officials, including the president of the United States and candidates for the presidency—is deeply unfair to the American people.

It is unfair precisely because it is wrong. People respond to public messages. Messages matter. And if all you hear from political leaders in both parties is that the game is rigged—that you are a victim of the elites and of immigrants, that you are largely helpless—then for many, that message will dim aspirations, reduce effort, and sap energy. And because the economy rewards hard work, if people aspire to less and put in less effort, their economic outcomes will suffer.

Instead, leaders should be presenting the true, fuller picture of American life and telling the American people that they should aspire to more, work harder, and face the future with confidence and energy. This message has the virtue of being true for the broad swath of Americans. And it will help people in our free society to use their freedom well, to realize their potential in the marketplace, and to find the dignity that comes with earned success.

The true picture better aligns with the national narrative—the story we tell about ourselves—that has helped to fuel prosperity and opportunity: All people have equal moral worth. Hard work is dignified. We are confident in the future, open to the world. We are not in a zero-sum conflict with each other; instead, my success can increase yours. We are a creedal nation, not an ethnic one. Our common culture is shaped by a shared dream—an American Dream—of better lives for ourselves and for our children.

STRENGTHENING THE DREAM

Messages matter, but they are not all that matters.

Strengthening the American Dream requires championing economic growth. The populist social irritant gets this wrong, so it is ironic that economic growth is itself a balm, promoting social harmony by allowing you to do better without requiring that your neighbor do worse.

Over the past several years, a growing economy and a tight labor market are leading businesses to hire workers they would have avoided interviewing in years past. Businesses are less likely to require criminal background checks in their job postings and seem to be hiring the formerly incarcerated at higher rates, and the employment rate for workers with disabilities has been increasing.

No employment program is as effective as a hot economy. And especially over the longer term, no policy change can match economic growth's effectiveness at raising the incomes of everyone in society. A rising tide does lift all boats, even if it does not lift them equally or at the same pace.

To keep the economy growing, policymakers should pursue a light regulatory regime and low tax rates. Productivity growth, and the higher wages that come with it, should be strengthened by encouraging savings and investment, and by increasing support for basic scientific research and innovation. Slow productivity growth is one of the most important economic challenges facing the United States. Policy should encourage entrepreneurship and economic dynamism, advance free trade and the efficiencies and productivity gains (and thus wage gains) it brings over time, increase high-skilled immigration, and put the national debt on a downward trajectory by reforming middle-class entitlement programs.

Economic opportunity and earned success are critical to

the American Dream, so public policy should work aggressively to increase labor force participation. More generous earnings subsidies can pull more people into the workforce and can lift the incomes of the working poor and working class. Relocation assistance targeted to long-term unemployed workers in struggling local labor markets can offer those workers a hand up to better employment opportunities.

Work-based learning programs, like apprenticeship programs, can build skills and increase wages by allowing market forces, rather than government bureaucrats, to determine which skills are taught to apprentices and can provide apprentices with marketable credentials. In general, community colleges can play a stronger role in skill building (for example, through career pathways, sectoral training, and traditional associate degrees that are targeted to marketable skills and specific occupations), but increased resources should be coupled with increased accountability for student outcomes. We need to ditch the "four-year college for all" mentality and replace it with an emphasis on marketable postsecondary skills and credentials, and lifelong learning training models. These sorts of programs, and not job training programs as currently designed, hold the promise to building skills and lifting wages for workers without college degrees.

Businesses can help, too. They have responsibilities to their workers and to society. Those that take the "high road"—investing in training their workers and building their skills—might find that doing so is not only good for workers but for their bottom lines as well.

Starting in elementary school, curriculum needs to be redesigned to match the realities of the 21st century economy. Technological automation will make emotional intelligence and creativity more valuable than solving routine problems, yet we still heavily prioritize the latter. Curriculum should emphasize skills that will complement technology, not skills that will place workers in competition with robots and software. The ability to collaborate and communicate will be key. In addition, school curricula need to emphasize more strongly career and technical education. To make sure future workers are competitive in the labor market, students should be in school for 12 months per year, not nine.

Beyond skills and training, commute times have become a barrier to opportunity in many large metro areas. Governments can help to mitigate this problem. Unnecessary regulation—like zoning and occupational licensing restrictions—is a barrier to labor market success in many communities. Disability insurance needs to be reformed to promote earned success in the labor market, and the safety net as a whole—including our unemployment insurance system—needs to be updated to make it a better launching pad for labor market success. Our incarceration policies and criminal justice system need to be reformed with future labor market outcomes in mind.

Underlying these policies are basic principles that can strengthen the American Dream: A strong commitment to individual liberty and the free enterprise system, and a commitment to advancing economic opportunity and personal responsibility. Support for a political economy in which markets create wealth and prosperity, some of which is redistributed or spent by a limited but energetic government to advance opportunity and to ensure socially desirable outcomes. A belief that the dignity of the human person is a central concern of public policy, that policy should advance the common good, and that we all share a special obligation to the poor and the vulnerable.

We need to fortify the American Dream in the face of real challenges. No one should seriously argue otherwise. But the Dream is certainly not dead, and we should not let a populist scream convince us otherwise.

That scream was more understandable in the depths of the Great Recession and the slow and uneven economic recovery from it. But it is time to set aside our fear of the future. It is time to set aside pessimism in favor of optimism.

It is the case that politicians and opinion leaders have fueled the narrative of pessimism, but that is partly because the American people respond to it with their votes, clicks, and views. This is a two-way street.

The American people should be optimistic because of the many reasons for optimism. That optimism should be a foundation for a renewal of energy and personal responsibility. The American Dream is alive, and it should breathe life into the American people. The American Dream is alive, but it requires hard work and asks all Americans for their contributions.

The American Dream is alive, and for that we should be grateful.

PART 2

---- ⋟⋞ ----

Dissenting Points of View

CHAPTER 11

Populism Isn't the Problem
It's a Response to Inequality

————————— ⋛⋚ —————————

E. J. DIONNE

DISSENT AND CRITICISM of conventional wisdom is always to be welcomed—even when you think the dissenter is wrong. Taking on prevailing opinion promotes debates that, ideally, clarify the situations in which we find ourselves and the choices we need to make.

But often, certain views take hold because they comport with both lived experiences and the data. So it is with the belief that the American Dream, as we have come to understand it, is in grave jeopardy, despite my friend Michael Strain's insistence in these pages that "the American Dream is alive, and for that we should be grateful."

Strain expresses alarm that "populists" might destroy the dream with misguided policies rooted in a misunderstanding of reality that greatly exaggerates the problems confronting members of the middle class (or those who aspire to join it) and the poor. He wants to persuade readers that the best way forward is to continue with the policies of the past, specifically those embodied in the Reagan economic consensus that is now under assault. You sense that the major purpose of Strain's effort is summarized in a single sentence near the end of this short book: "To keep the economy growing, policymakers should pursue a light regulatory regime and low tax rates." If contemporary capitalism is as successful as Strain claims, it would seem axiomatic that what we need is an even stronger dose of it.

Alas, for those who think that Reaganism is still the answer, Strain's argument is flawed in three fundamental ways. First, he misstates the claims of those who are critical of the current economy. Second, he misses the long story of the decline of the American Dream by trying to focus our attention on a much narrower timeframe. Third, he ignores the deteriorating bargaining power of wage earners that has led to a significant drop in their share of the nation's wealth and income.

The American Dream will not be worthy of the name as long as our social mobility rates lag well behind those of many more egalitarian European nations.[51] And our market economy will continue to arouse widespread popular suspicion as long as opportunities to accumulate wealth are skewed radically toward those who are already very wealthy and who enjoy outsized influence over the workings of our democratic system.

Before turning to these issues, however, I pause to honor

Strain for confronting the damage the Trump presidency has done to our country. Unlike Strain, I do not see Trump as an authentic populist but instead as a phony. His economic policies have largely benefitted the privileged and have, indeed, followed the path of deregulation and tax cutting—for the best off, it should be said—that Strain recommends. But Strain is right to call out Trump for badly damaging the post–World War II international order, for demonizing immigrants, and, especially, "for stoking racial animosity." He is right that Trump's shameful approach to race "threatens the American Dream . . . the way termites threaten the integrity of a house—by rotting its very core." Not enough conservatives have the courage to say this as plainly and directly as Strain does. Good for him.

And Strain is not indifferent to social injustices. Some of his proposals, including calls for expanded "earnings subsidies," relocation assistance for the unemployed, and far greater use of apprenticeship programs would find wide support among progressives (including progressive populists). His gratuitous attack on "government bureaucrats" undercuts his case, since all these programs would necessarily involve partnerships between government and the private sector. Who but "bureaucrats" would take responsibility for managing the government side? Nonetheless, I suspect that beneath his rhetoric, Strain knows this perfectly well.

Strain's tendency toward rhetorical excess may be relatively harmless in this instance, but it also undermines the broader argument he is trying to make as he introduces us to regiments of straw men and straw women.

Early on, he writes, "Precisely because hard work pays off and people can successfully climb the economic ladder, telling people that they cannot hurts their outcomes by sapping their energy and diminishing their aspirations."

And he offers this ringing denunciation that conflates "populists" on all sides of politics.

"Both the populist left and right are turning inward," he writes, "anxious about the future, closed to the world, attempting to return to an imagined past, intoxicated with nostalgia or with the concept of an unattainable utopian future. And both, he adds, "are retreating from the importance of personal responsibility, embracing a narrative of victimhood."

I will not pretend to speak for the right, but the claim that progressives are denigrating work or denying the value of aspiration is a fiction. The core argument that progressives are making is precisely that work *is* deeply honorable and valuable, and that increasing social mobility—meaning the capacity to get ahead through effort and creativity—should be a central goal of public policy. In presidential politics, those making the case for what Senator Sherrod Brown has called "the dignity of work" include everyone from both the left (among them, figures Strain might call "populist") and the center-left: from Elizabeth Warren, Bernie Sanders, and Julian Castro to Joe Biden, Pete Buttigieg, Amy Klobuchar,

Corey Booker, and Michael Bennett. What they are arguing is that for Americans in large numbers, the rewards from work are not what they should be. Far from being "utopian," they all stand in the practical tradition of American social reform going back to the New Deal.

If progressives were claiming that the American economy has collapsed into a great heap and that absolutely nothing good has happened for 50 years, Strain's argument might make sense. But no one on the left is saying this. Nor does the left deny the benefits of the revolutionary innovations wrought by technological change. What they insist upon is that the fruits of this transformation should be distributed equitably, and that the bargaining power of Americans negatively affected by it should be enhanced. Here, for example, is what Warren, who takes the brunt of some of Strain's attacks, said when she offered a plan to protect the rights of workers in the gig economy in 2016: "Massive technological change is a gift—a byproduct of human ingenuity that creates extraordinary opportunities to improve the lives of billions. But history shows that to harness those opportunities to create and sustain a strong middle class, policy also matters. To fully realize the potential of this new economy, laws must be adapted to make sure that the basic bargain for workers remains intact, and that workers have the chance to share in the growth they help produce."[52]

These are not the words of a utopian, a nostalgist, or a Luddite.

I will leave it to Strain's fellow economists to argue with him over whether he uses the right measures of inflation to gauge income changes, over the difference studying "average wages" or "median wages" and other issues of this sort. They obviously matter to his argument, as Strain, to his credit, acknowledges when, for example, he challenges the conclusions Raj Chetty and his colleagues offer in their important paper, "The Fading American Dream."

But it is striking that Strain wants us to focus on what has happened since 1990 and to forget about everything that came before. He gives the game away when he writes: "Why should a politician, a commentator, or a worker care how much wages have grown since 1973? That was 46 years ago. Very few of today's workers were in the labor force that long ago."

This is the polemical equivalent of "pay no attention to the man behind the curtain." Strain thus conveniently begins the conversation long after the end of the post–World War II social bargain, on which the very idea of the American Dream was built. It's revealing that he picks 1973, when the march of economic inequality began. It took off in in earnest after 1980, and Strain clearly does not want us to question the regressive policies of the Reagan era, the effects of which are still with us. He hopes we will forget that we once had a more egalitarian form of capitalism in which unions were strong, the bargaining power of workers was substantial, taxes were more progressive, the financial sector was far less dominant, and economic growth lifted all quintiles more or less equally.

The longer view is deeply damaging to the argument that Strain is trying to make. For example, Jay Shambaugh and Ryan Nunn of the Brookings Institution's Hamilton Project (hardly a bastion of "populism," by the way) showed in the *Harvard Business Review* in 2017 that labor's share of the nation's income fell from "nearly 65 percent in the mid-1970s to below 57 percent in 2017." The result? "Since the early 1970s, the hourly inflation-adjusted wages received by the typical worker have barely risen, growing only 0.2 percent per year," they write. "In other words, though the economy has been growing, the primary way most people benefit from that growth has almost completely stalled."[53]

Similarly, Lawrence Mishel, Elise Gould, and Josh Bivens of the Economic Policy Institute demonstrated that the longer view shows the degree to which productivity gains are now disconnected from wage growth. They note that in the three decades following World War II, "hourly compensation of the vast majority of workers rose 91 percent, roughly in line with productivity growth of 97 percent." But "for most of the past generation, (except for a brief period in the late 1990s), pay for the vast majority lagged further and further behind overall productivity." Between 1973 and 2013, they conclude, "hourly compensation for a typical (production/nonsupervisory worker) rose just 9 percent while productivity increased 74 percent."

The difference between the current economy and the economy in the roughly three decades after World War II—which is to say the difference between the American Dream economy and what we have now—can be summarized by this finding from Mishel and his colleagues about the impact of rising inequality: "In 2007, the last year before the Great Recession, the average income of the middle 60 percent of American households was $76,443. It would have been $94,310, roughly 23 percent (nearly $18,000) higher had inequality not widened."[54]

Of course, the world has changed since the decades after World War II. The shared growth of that era unleashed a revolution of rising expectations that helped prompt the civil rights and feminist movements. No one pretends that we can restore the world exactly as it was in, say, 1964, and there are many reasons why we would not want to—among them, the ways in which the struggles for racial and gender equality have made us a better nation.

But between the more social form of capitalism that the New Deal economic consensus helped create and the more radical form unleashed in the Reagan era, it is the more social form that made the American Dream possible. The Reagan consensus is collapsing because a majority of Americans know that we need to make capitalism fairer and more inclusive. Pretending that its current form is working better than it is won't get us to the next stage that will adapt ideas rooted in social market and social democratic insights to our new circumstances.

Strain writes that his essay is "not a call to complacency." Knowing him, I know he means it. That's why I hope he turns his intellectual gifts and his strong moral sense from defending a status quo that is falling short to the work of creating a more just and dynamic alternative.

CHAPTER 12

Why Economic Trends Support Conservative Populism

— ≥≤ —

HENRY OLSEN

MICHAEL STRAIN does an excellent job of disproving the common tropes of American economic decline. Many Americans are getting ahead. Inequality growth is slowing down. Employment growth is high, remarkably so when compared to many other advanced Western democracies.

This does not, however, mean he refutes the conservative populist argument. A close examination of his own data shows some worrying facts about the labor market and wage stagnation that support the conservative populist critique.

Strain also overlooks some important factors, such as the changes in educational attainment, the recent growth in minimum wage increases, the number of hours worked by adults in a household, and regional differences in employment and economic growth. Taking these into account might, and likely would, show why conservative populism has an audience.

Finally, Strain presents a cartoon version of the conservative populist critique of modern capitalism. Cherry-picking the worst aspects of President Trump's philosophy does not do justice to the arguments Republican Senators Marco Rubio or Josh Hawley make. It also overlooks the degree to which Trump's own policies may have contributed to the very recent gains Strain lauds.

In short, conservative populism remains a viable argument that serious defenders of American liberal democratic capitalism need to consider if they want the great engine of human advancement to both survive and continue to work for almost all Americans.

CRACKS IN STRAIN'S EDIFICE: WHAT THE DATA SHOW

Strain contends his data show a largely rosy picture for most Americans regarding employment and wage growth. But his data point to some disturbing trends that suggest many people are not benefitting or have not benefitted much until very recently.

His data on the labor market are one example. Figure 1 shows the prime-age labor force participation rates for men and women. Despite a rise among men since 2014–2015, participation rates for 25- to 54-year-old men remain about 8 percent lower today than they were in 1960. There are roughly 55.6 million men in that group; an 8 percent decline in labor market participation means nearly 4.5 million men who should be trying to get a job are not. That's a huge problem.

The data are also consistent with the conservative populists' narrative regarding declining opportunities for men with lower educational attainment. Participation rate declines are choppy, with periods of decline alternating with periods of stability. The declining periods roughly coincide with periods of known deindustrialization, times when recessions and global competition forced outmoded factories to close down. This suggests that some men have failed to find their way back into the labor force after each period of adjustment despite the overall trend of rising wages and opportunity. More research is needed, but I suspect one will find that certain groups of men become unemployable after these downturns and drop out of a labor market that has no use for them. This is exactly what Senator Rubio is referring to in the quote Strain uses in the book's introduction.

The same issue arises in figure 3, which measures labor market dynamism. All three measures in that figure decline after 2001, which is when China acceded to the World Trade Organization. This is consistent with the thesis that Chinese industrial competition has forced millions of Americans out of their manufacturing jobs and thus has lowered job prospects for a large and crucial segment of American workers.[55]

Other data from Strain's book point to Chinese competition as a significant, yet underexplored, phenomenon in America's recent economic and social history. Figure 4 shows that the suicide rate starts to increase in 2001.

Figure 5 shows that the long-term unemployment rate has been higher since 2001 than in any preceding time period even at its low points. How curious.

Strain's data also show that wage stagnation was very real for the decade before the 2016 election. Figure 9 shows real wages increased for the bottom half of the earnings distribution between 1996 and 2003, and then stagnated even during the expansion of the 2000s until roughly 2014. Combined with the data above, this means Americans in the bottom half of the skills matrix experienced decreased employment opportunities and stagnating wages for those with jobs for nearly a decade. No wonder they were open to "populist" messages!

Other data supports this argument. Figure 10 shows that real median market income adjusted for family size steadily increased during the 1990s but then dropped during the two recessions, such that it only exceeded its 2001 peak in 2014. Rising cash subsidies and tax cuts from the government made up the market deficiency, but even those measures failed to sustain consumption between 2007 and 2013. The message is clear: the welfare state and targeted tax cuts compensated for market failure for the better part of 15 years.

WHY THE "GOOD NEWS" MAY NOT BE SO GOOD

Even Strain's good news is likely overstated compared to many Americans' expectations and underlying preferences. Take the shift in the nature of middle-skill, middle-income jobs since the 1970s. Strain argues that the shift away from production-based "old middle" jobs toward personal service-based "new middle jobs," depicted in figure 14, shows a healthy economy. But what if you were a 45-year-old male laid off from a factory "old middle" job in 2004? You likely don't have the interpersonal skills or educational background to qualify for the "new middle" jobs Strain describes. Your options are thus to work in what the low-wage jobs the economy will provide for you or drop out of the labor force entirely. Many people might choose the low-wage alternative, but that doesn't mean they are happy. This discontent has political effects economists like Strain overlook.

This pattern—overlooking a person's expectations and actual opportunities—pervades Strain's argument. We know, for example, that educational attainment has increased significantly in the last five decades. But nowhere does Strain adjust for education attainment when looking at median household income or employment statistics. Failing to do that likely hides the very real "apples-to-apples" comparison between people of similar educational backgrounds over time. There are fewer prime-aged working Americans who have never completed at least a two-year college degree than there were 30 years ago, so it makes sense that the median household is doing better in an economy that rewards higher skills. But the person who doesn't obtain those skills, perhaps because they lack the intellectual capacity to succeed in higher education programs, likely faces much worse economic outcomes than a similarly situated person in 1990. That is the comparison real people in such circumstances are making, and that is the comparison that makes "populism" politically attractive.

The same is true for other factors Strain ignores. He finds incomes going up once adjusted for household size, but some people might not want to forego an extra child because they can't afford to raise one when saving for college is a necessity rather than a luxury. A household might be getting by but be upset about the decline in their community sparked by economic dislocation. Household income might be going up at the bottom because of recent large minimum wage increases, not market forces.[56] Household income might be sustained because of female labor force participation even when the woman might prefer to be at home. All of these considerations would have strong political ramifications, but Strain's rosy scenario ignores them entirely.

Conservative Populism Isn't about Trump

Strain departs from his data when he turns to discuss Trump. He equates Trump's positions on foreign policy, entitlement spending, protectionism, and anti-immigrant rhetoric with those of conservative populists generally even though no one I know in that movement shares these views. He says Trump's rhetoric matters because "people respond to public messages," yet fails to consider whether Trump's pro-worker rhetoric perhaps has contributed to the addition of more than 500,000 manufacturing jobs in the United States since his election, reversing a decades-long trend, or to the increase in wage growth that mysteriously coincides in time with Trump's victory (Strain, 27).[57] Strain's last chapter says more about his dislike of Trump than it does about conservative populism.

Conservative populism in the real world is nothing more than an argument that new times require new measures. Those of us who are part of this movement believe that some types of people and some regions of America are not benefitting from the modern economy. We believe it is the proper role of government to try to ameliorate those conditions, much as American government has used public power since the days of the Whig Party to encourage broad economic growth and widespread prosperity. We are not bigots, protectionists, or spendthrifts, as our adversaries want to paint us. We are, however, not free-market fundamentalists who instinctively say "no" to any serious proposal to exercise public power for the public benefit.

The real debate on the right is not between troglodyte Trumpism and a magical capitalist Nirvana. It is instead between two well-meaning groups of conservatives. One side contends the modern American economy does not unintentionally cause serious problems for tens of millions of people, or that it is morally improper for the federal government to act even if it does. The other side contends there are serious economic problems that threaten our country's social and political fabric and that it is morally justifiable, if not imperative, for us to act.

Strain's book effectively refutes the "left populist" argument of general capitalist failure. It does not, however, come to grips with the real conservative populist argument or the facts behind it. As a result, it falls far short of closing down the debate on the right. Indeed, it stokes it.

CHAPTER 13

A Response to E. J. Dionne and Henry Olsen

≳≲

MICHAEL R. STRAIN

I'M VERY GRATEFUL to Henry Olsen and E. J. Dionne for their responses and reactions to my book. I invited my friends Henry and E. J. to provide responses because they are two of the sharpest and most knowledgeable analysts of these issues, and I knew we would disagree on fundamental points. My hope is that the contrast will sharpen my arguments for the reader.

In my brief response to them, I will analyze select points of disagreement that highlight where fundamental differences between us exist. I won't address all points of disagreement, and I won't spend much time on areas of agreement, except to say that I am grateful those exist and am grateful to them for their generosity in pointing them out.

Olsen offers an energetic defense of conservative populism in his response. The first two-thirds of his essay illustrate precisely the tendency among supporters of populism that I argue is unhelpful and a disservice to the American people: highlighting pockets of (actual, serious) problems and confusing them for the common experience of typical people in the United States today.

It's important to say clearly that Olsen is right about many (but certainly not all) of the problems he cites. Take three examples. As I argue in this book, people and towns left behind by economic transitions, the economic outcomes and opportunities available to workers who have dropped out of high school, and deaths of despair are all very real problems that demand serious policy responses and national attention.

But relatively few places have been left behind. This is not the impression an informed observer would get by reading Olsen's response, or from the public debate more generally. According to a 2018 Brookings report, 62 percent of U.S. counties identified as having a disproportionately large share of manufacturing jobs in 1970 have successfully transitioned to new industries, and 22 percent exhibited strong or emerging economic performance over the past two decades while still having a large manufacturing sector intact.[58]

In his inaugural address, President Trump described an "American carnage" of "rusted-out factories scattered like tombstones across the landscape of our nation."[59] This populist characterization is inaccurate. Few towns have been devastated by deindustrialization.

Similarly, the common experience of Americans is to have some postsecondary education. It isn't to be without a high school diploma. Only 10 percent of American adults have less than a high school education.[60] And every death of despair is a tragedy. Though there are far too many such deaths, they remain far from the common experience.

Public policy should absolutely do more to bring economic opportunity to people in these situations. But these situations should not drive the national policy agenda into an embrace of protectionism and hostility toward immigrants that will be detrimental to the long-term economic health of the country—and to them.

Olsen claims that I "overlook" people's expectations. To the contrary, I argue that they are of central importance, and that the populist message of economic and social despair is miscalibrating expectations to the detriment of the American people. I also argue that the populist impulse to deny people agency and to treat them as victims—which exhibits itself in parts of Olsen's response—is counterproductive.

There is no doubt, to use Olsen's example, that a 45-year-old man laid off from a factory faces a serious challenge. The message opinion leaders and elected officials should be sending him is that he can get back on his feet and spend the next two decades of his career as a successful wage earner in a new job. This is not just happy talk—the evidence presented throughout this book suggests that with hard work, he can achieve this outcome. Like all of us, he has a responsibility to earn his own success, and he is capable of doing exactly that. This is not to minimize the significant challenge he faces. Instead, it is to place that challenge in an accurate context.

Olsen argues that I do not "do justice to the arguments"

Marco Rubio makes, despite quoting him as an example of a conservative who argues that the American Dream is in great peril. I agree with Olsen on this point. A detailed exploration of Senator Rubio's views on these issues and of his policy agenda is outside the scope of this book. But, as I argue in the second chapter, I do believe the senator is incorrect in his public statements on the American Dream and related matters.

I say that despite the enthusiasm I have for some of Senator Rubio's specific policy proposals and recent approach to these issues. For example, the senator's emphasis on workers as a central concern of public policy is refreshing from a Republican, and right on target. It is an example of how the populist impulse can be channeled productively.

According to Olsen, I equate "Trump's positions on foreign policy, entitlement spending, protectionism, and anti-immigrant rhetoric with those of conservative populists generally even though no one" he knows "in that movement shares these views." This is a puzzling sentence. The president's views on these issues have permeated the Republican Party, conservative media and publications, and important conservative institutions. It may be that support for Trumpian populism on some of these issues is half-an-inch deep. But the political right, the conservative entertainment establishment, and much of the conservative intelligentsia today find themselves in the president's corner on all of this.

Olsen concludes by saying that "conservative populism in

the real world is nothing more than an argument that new times require new measures." This is not the case. It is much more than that.

Of course new times require new measures. Of course government needs to do more to advance economic opportunity to those who need it most. My disagreement with Olsen is not about political philosophy or the wisdom of "market fundamentalism" as a guide to public policy. My disagreement is not theoretical. It is about the harmful way that populism on the political right has manifested itself—in the real world—during the past several years.

Olsen writes: "Strain's book effectively refutes the 'left populist' argument of general capitalist failure." E. J. Dionne disagrees. Dionne argues that I engage in rhetorical excess in my description of the progressive left. "If progressives were claiming that the American economy has collapsed into a great heap and that absolutely nothing good has happened for 50 years," he writes, "Strain's argument might make sense. But no one on the left is saying this."

No one on the left may be saying that "absolutely nothing good has happened" since 1970. But it would be difficult to listen to the leading voices on the left in the last three or four years and not to walk away with the conclusion that economic outcomes for the majority of Americans have been declining rapidly over the past several decades. (Bernie Sanders: "For many, the American dream has become a nightmare.") Dionne himself refers to "the long story of the decline of the American Dream" in his essay. My purpose in this book is to argue that there is not a long story of decline.

Dionne criticizes my argument that some on the progressive left deny the importance of personal responsibility, the value of work, and the benefits of technological innovations. Yet railing against the elites as the source of most economic challenges and arguing that the "game is rigged" do seem to deny people agency and responsibility. Dismissing the jobs held by millions of Americans as "bad jobs" and telling people that hard work won't pay off do suggest that much work is not properly valued. Arguing to break up the major technology companies that produce revolutionary innovation seems to suggest its benefits are not terribly important.

In the book I argue that wages and incomes have not been stagnant for decades. I calculate growth from 1990 to the present to substantiate this. Dionne takes issue with my deemphasizing the decades that came before 1990. He writes: "Strain clearly does not want us to question the regressive policies of the Reagan era."

Let me first acknowledge (as I do in chapter 6) that the best starting year for these sorts of comparisons is not obvious, and reasonable people can disagree. I provide several pages of argument in favor of using 1990, which I won't repeat here.

Dionne refers to my focus on the 30 years since 1990 as "the polemical equivalent of 'pay no attention to the man behind the curtain,'" and argues that "the longer view is deeply damaging to the argument that Strain is trying to make." But looking further back does not alter my conclusions. Take two years Dionne highlights in his response, 1973 and 1980. As reported in the book, the average wage of typical workers (i.e., nonsupervisory and production workers) has increased by 23 percent since 1973.[61] Average wages have grown by 29 percent since 1980. (They have increased by 49 percent since 1964, as well.) Median household income after taxes and government transfers increased by 64 percent between 1980 and 2016, the last year for which CBO data are available.

These are solid increases. They are not spectacular. They are slower than growth for the top 1 percent. We should not be satisfied with this pace of wage and income growth. New and better public policies are needed to help workers command higher wages in the labor market.

But this increase represents significant growth in purchasing power for typical households. Steady annual gains have accumulated into a solid increase in wages and incomes for typical households. This is not stagnant wage and income growth—wages and income have not stagnated for decades.

A final point: the graph above is the same as figure 6 in the main body of this book. As I argue in chapter 6, it is reasonable to break this figure up into three periods: a period of wage growth from the mid-1960s until the mid-1970s; stagnant and declining wages from the mid-1970s until the mid-1990s; and growth since the mid-1990s.

FIGURE 22. AVERAGE REAL WAGE FOR PRODUCTION
AND NONSUPERVISORY EMPLOYEES.

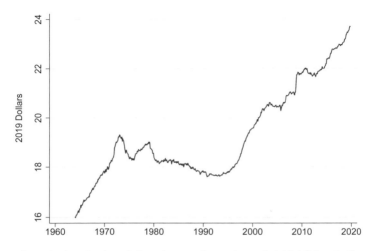

Average hourly earnings for production and nonsupervisory employees adjusted for inflation using the
personal consumption expenditures price index.

Source: Bureau of Labor Statistics and Bureau of Economic Analysis data retrieved from FRED;
author's calculations.

So the type of simple comparison between the 1970s and
today that Dionne wants to make is incomplete. Instead,
it's better to acknowledge the behavior of wages in each
of these periods. Have wages been stagnant since the early
1970s? No. Wages stagnated from the mid-1970s until the
mid-1990s, and then they began a period of increase that has
continued to the present day.

That period of increase—not stagnation—characterizes the past several decades.

Dionne makes an excellent point that we would not want to "restore the world exactly as it was in, say, 1964" in part because of "the ways in which the struggles [since then] for racial and gender equality have made us a better nation." Absolutely correct. This is one of many reasons why populist nostalgia for life decades ago is misplaced and should be resisted.

Dionne argues that my goal is "to persuade readers that the best way forward is to continue with the policies of the past." "If contemporary capitalism is as successful as Strain claims," he writes, "it would seem axiomatic that what we need is an even stronger dose of it."

Contemporary capitalism has been very successful, as this short book demonstrates. We do need a stronger dose of it, if by "it" Dionne means stronger incentives in public policy to work and invest, more risk-taking, more basic research, more energy and dynamism.

But as I write in chapter 10, this is not all we need. We need to address the serious pockets of problems that have captured national attention. We need a strong social safety net to ensure that in a nation as rich as ours no one falls too far. We need better policies to advance economic opportunity. We need businesses to meet their responsibilities to their workers. We need workers to meet the challenges they face with confidence that they can succeed.

The storm clouds of the Great Recession have passed. It is time to set aside pessimism in favor of optimism because of the many reasons there are to be optimistic.

The American Dream is alive, and for that we should be grateful.

Acknowledgments

⋙⋘

I AM EXTREMELY GRATEFUL TO Susan Arellano, publisher of Templeton Press. Susan was a wonderful companion at every stage of this project. As an editor, her candid and clear feedback was as helpful as it was refreshing. Her team at Templeton, including Trish Vergilio and Dan Reilly, was enormously helpful in the scramble to get this book across the finish line.

If it weren't for the outstanding research support of Duncan Hobbs this book would still be in its first draft. Duncan is a talented young social scientist who has become a master of economic data and analysis. He read every page of this book more than once, making excellent suggestions along the way. I spoke with Duncan about the ideas and arguments in this book, and it is much better for those conversations. (Any errors in this book are mine alone.) I am also very grateful to Maryanna Mitchell, who manages my office and coordinated AEI's work on this book. Maryanna allowed me to focus on the creative side of this project, confident that everything else would turn out perfectly. She learned much from her predecessor Adele Hunter, to whom I also owe much gratitude.

Robert Doar, the president of AEI, has been extremely supportive of me and of this work. I am very grateful to him, and to all the staff members at AEI whose time and talents have made this project more successful. I am deeply indebted to Arthur Brooks, who encouraged me for years to write a book and whose example and friendship I will always treasure. AEI has been my intellectual home for many years. The scholars at AEI are wonderful colleagues and friends, and learning from them every day is a great gift and pleasure. AEI has given much more to me than I have contributed to it. Especially in our current political moment, it is an indispensable institution.

I thank conference participants at Harvard and the University of Wisconsin for helpful feedback on an earlier version of this project. Some sections of the fifth chapter of this book draw on an essay I wrote for the *Guardian* in June 2019, and some sections of the sixth chapter draw on a paper I published with the Aspen Institute in February 2019. Several of the arguments in this book received their first airing by me in my Bloomberg colum.

I owe the most to my lovely wife, Carolyne. I would never have been able to finish this book on schedule without her support, patience, and encouragement. She endured too many nights and weekends with me holed up in the study working on this project. Carolyne is a wonderful mother to our two children. This book is dedicated to them.

Notes

─────────────── ≥≤ ───────────────

1. *New York Times* (@nytimes). "We covered the whole history of lawns." Twitter, August 9, 2019.

2. Samuel J. Abrams, et al., "AEI Survey on Community and Society: Social Capital, Civic Health, and Quality of Life in the United States," American Enterprise Institute, February 2019..

3. Donald Trump, "Presidential Campaign Announcement." Campaign speech, Trump Tower, New York, NY, June 15, 2015.

4. Senator Bernie Sanders (@SenSanders). "American workers are some of the most overworked yet our standard of living has fallen. For many, the American dream has become a nightmare." Twitter, May 17, 2016, 12:46pm.

5. Senator Marco Rubio, "America Needs to Restore Dignity of Work," *Atlantic*. December 13, 2018.

6. Senator Elizabeth Warren and Mayor Bill de Blasio, "How to Revive the American Dream," *Washington Post*. May 6, 2015.

7. "Senator Hawley Delivers the Commencement Address at The King's College," May 13, 2019, at 11:45, https://www.youtube.com /watch?v=WPNNVnRHrxQ&feature=youtu.be.

8 Tucker Carlson, "The American Dream is dying," streamed on January 3, 2019, https://www.youtube.com/watch?v=mgvpxE_WKxw.

9. Joseph E. Stiglitz, "Progressive Capitalism Is Not an Oxymoron." *New York Times*. April 19, 2019.

10. Ray Dalio, interviewed by Bill Whittaker, "Ray Dalio says wealth inequality is a national emergency," *60 Minutes*. July 28, 2019.

11. John Paul II, *Laborem Exercens*, 1981.

12. Steven J. Davis and John Haltiwanger, "Labor Market Fluidity and Economic Performance," NBER Working Paper No. 20479, September 2014.

13. Jennifer Steinhauer, "A Worker Shortage Is Forcing Restaurants to Get Creative," *New York Times*, April 5, 2018.

14. Burning Glass Technologies, "Fewer Job Postings Demanded Background Checks in 2017," Labor Market Analysis, January 23, 2018.

15. Rachel Abrams, "7 Fast-Food Chains to End 'No Poach' Deals That Lock Down Low-Wage Workers," *New York Times*, July 12, 2018.

16. Alan B. Krueger and Orley Ashenfelter, "Theory and Evidence on Employer Collusion in the Franchise Sector," NBER Working Paper No. 24831, July 2018.

17. Matt Marx, "Reforming Non-Competes to Support Workers," The Hamilton Project, Policy Proposal 2018-04, February 2018.

18. Janna E. Johnson and Morris M. Kleiner, "Is Occupational Licensing a Barrier to Interstate Migration?," NBER Working Paper No. 24017, December 2017.

19. Board of Governors of the Federal Reserve System, "Monetary Policy Report Submitted to Congress on February 17, 2000, Pursuant to the Full Employment and Balanced Growth Act of 1978: Monetary Policy and the Economic Outlook (section 1)."

20 The CPI-U-RS value for 2019 was not released at the time of writing, so all direct comparisons between wages deflated by this measure and the PCE take 2018 as the end year.

21. The data used to generate this graph are generously made available by the Economic Policy Institute on its website. The data come from the CPS-MORG.

22. Anna M. Stansbury and Lawrence H. Summers, "Productivity and Pay: Is the Link Broken?," NBER Working Paper No. 24165, December 2017.

23. Income figures for the bottom 20 percent are not adjusted for household size. Income figures for median household income are adjusted for household size. The CBO does not have size-adjusted measures available for the bottom 20 percent.

24. U.S. Energy Information Administration, "Air Conditioning in Nearly 100 Million Homes," Residential Energy Consumption Survey: Analysis and Projections, August 19, 2011.

25. U.S. Department of Education, National Center for Education Statistics. (2019). The Condition of Education 2019 (NCES 2019-144), Educational Attainment of Young Adults.

26. Robert B. Avery, et al., "Survey of Consumer Finances, 1983: A Second Report," *Federal Reserve Bulletin*, 70 (December 1984), 857–68.

27. Jesse Bricker, et al., "Changes in US family finances from 2013 to 2016: Evidence from the Survey of Consumer Finances." *Federal Reserve Bulletin*, 103 (2017): 1.

28. Robert J. Gordon, *The Rise and Fall of American Growth: The US Standard of Living Since the Civil War.* Vol. 70. Princeton University Press, 2017, 484.

29. Gordon, 464.

30. Centers for Disease Control, Age-adjusted death rates for selected causes of death, by sex, race, and Hispanic origin: United States, selected years 1950–2017 (Trend Tables). Health United States–2018.

31. Gordon, 471.

32. Gordon, 455.

33. Gordon, 400.

34. Steven Pinker, *Enlightenment Now: The Case for Reason, Science, Humanism, and Progress.* Penguin, 2018, 59.

35. Pinker, 251.

36. Pinker, 251.

37. Pinker, 256.

38. Pinker, 257.

39. Susanna Locke, "You're Less Likely to Die in a Car Crash Nowadays – Here's Why." *Vox*. Published April 6, 2014. Accessed October 19, 2018.s

40. *CNN Newsroom*, "Sen. Elizabeth Warren Announces Candidacy for President at Massachusetts Rally; Caravan Awaits at Eagle Pass, Texas, to Cross Border," aired 12–1pm ET, February 9, 2019.

41. Senator Josh Hawley (@HawleyMO). 2019. "It calls out their alliance with the multinational corporations, their devaluaing of American labor, . . . ," Twitter, July 20, 2019.

42. David H. Autor, "Work of the Past, Work of the Future," Richard T. Ely Lecture, AEA Papers and Proceedings 109 (2019): 1–32.

43. William D. Nordhaus, "Two Centuries of Productivity Growth in Computing," *Journal of Economic History*, 67, no. 1 (March 2007): 128–59.

44. Harry Holzer, "Job Market Polarization and U.S. Worker Skills: A Tale of Two Middles," Economic Studies at Brookings, April 2015.

45. Income statistics are taken from the U.S. Census Bureau's report, "Income and Poverty in the United States: 2018." Income is defined as money income received before taxes, and not including noncash government benefits. Income is adjusted for inflation by the Census Bureau using the CPI-U-RS.

46. Technical details: I use data from the 1968–2017 waves of the PSID, keeping individuals who were between the ages of 40 and 49 in 2013, 2015, and 2017. I use this tight age range to control for life cycle effects, which results in a relatively small number of observations. I have done all the analysis using the broader age range of 35–55 as well, and the results are qualitatively similar. I use the SRC and SEO samples, but not the immigrant subsample. I adjust income for inflation using the PCE, and for household size by dividing by the square root of household size. I use the longitudinal weights for the analysis. To ensure that I am capturing a measure of permanent income, I drop individuals who are missing more than two child income observations or more than four parent income observations (this discrepancy is due to the PSID's switch to biannual interviews in 1997).

47. The economic mobility statistics presented in the main text are estimated on a sample of people in their 40s. Using a broader age group increases the number of observations used to generate the statistics. The results presented in the text are qualitatively similar to those from a sample including people ages 35—55. With the larger sample, 76 percent of children have higher family incomes than their parents as adults. Eighty-six percent of children raised in the bottom 20 percent go on to have higher incomes than their parents. Eighty-three percent raised in the second quintile do, as well. Median parent income is approximately $34,000 in this larger sample, and median income of their children when their children are adults (i.e., of today's adults) is about $51,000.

48. Raj Chetty, David Grusky, Maximilian Hell, Nathaniel Hendren, Robert Manduca, and Jimmy Narang, "The Fading American Dream: Trends in Absolute Income Mobility Since 1940," *Science*, vol. 356, no. 6336, 2017.

49. Scott Winship, "Economic Mobility in America: A State-of-the-Art Primer," Archbridge Institute, Contemporary Levels of Mobility, March 2017.

50. As with family income, earnings mobility statistics are qualitatively similar when calculated using the broader age range of 35–55. Overall, 58 percent of today's men in that age range earn more than their fathers did when their fathers were 35–55 years old. Seventy-eight and 61 percent of sons raised in the bottom and second quintiles, respectively, went on to out earn their fathers. Median labor earnings for sons is approximately $62,000 and for fathers is approximately $56,000.

51. OECD, "*A Broken Social Elevator? How to Promote Social Mobility*," Published June 15, 2018.

52. Elizabeth Warren, United States Senator for Massachusetts, "Senator Warren Lays Out Steps to Protect Workers in the 'Gig Economy,'" speech given May 19, 2016.

53. Jay Schambaugh and Ryan Nunn, "Why Wages Aren't Growing in America," Brookings Institution, November 14, 2017.

54. Lawrence Mishel, Elise Gould, and Josh Bivens, "Wage Stagnation in Nine Charts," Economic Policy Institute, January 6, 2015.

55. David H. Autor, David Dorn, and Gordon H. Hanson, "The China Syndrome: Local Labor Market Effects of Import Competition in the United States," *American Economic Review* (2013) 103, no. 6.

56. National Conference of State Legislatures, "State Minimum Wages: 2019 Minimum Wage by State," January 6, 2019.

57. FRED Economic Data, "All Employees, Manufacturing," December 6, 2019; Heather Long, "U.S. Has Lost 5 Million Manufacturing Jobs Since 2000," *CNN Business*, March 29, 2016.

58. Alan Berube and Cecile Murray, "Renewing America's Economic Promise through Older Industrial Cities," Brookings Institution, April 2018.

59. Donald J. Trump, "The Inaugural Address," White House, January 20, 2017.

60. "Educational Attainment in the United States: 2018," U.S. Census Bureau, February 21, 2019.

61. In chapter 6, I report 21 percent growth since 1973. Wages grew 21 percent between 1973 and 2018 and 23 percent between 1973 and 2019. I stop in 2018 in the main text in order to make an apples-to-apples comparison with wages deflated by the CPI-U-RS, which is only available through 2018. Here, I use the most recent data available at the time of writing.

About the Contributors

✺

E. J. DIONNE JR. is a *Washington Post* columnist, professor at Georgetown University's McCourt School of Public Policy, a senior fellow at the Brookings Institution, and a visiting professor at Harvard University. His latest book is *Code Red: How Progressives and Moderates Can Unite to Save Our Country* (St. Martin's Press, 2020).

HENRY OLSEN is currently a Senior Fellow at the Ethics and Public Policy Center and a columnist at the *Washington Post*. He has worked in senior executive positions at many center-right think tanks. Olsen served as vice president and director of the National Research Initiative at the American Enterprise Institute from 2006 to 2013. He previously worked as vice president of programs at the Manhattan Institute and as president of the Commonwealth Foundation. Mr. Olsen's work has been featured in many prominent publications, including the *New York Times,* the *Wall Street Journal,* the *Washington Post*, the *Guardian, National Review,* and the *Weekly Standard*. He is the author of *Ronald Reagan: New Deal Conservative* (HarperCollins, 2017) and coauthor (with Dante J. Scala) of *The Four Faces of the Republican Party: The Fight for the 2016 Presidential Nomination* (Palgrave Macmillan, 2016).

About the Author

≥≤

MICHAEL R. STRAIN is director of Economic Policy Studies and resident scholar at the American Enterprise Institute. An economist, his research has been published in academic and policy journals and he has edited two books on economics and public policy. He is a research fellow at the Institute of Labor Economics (IZA) in Bonn, Germany, writes regularly for popular audiences, and is a columnist for *Bloomberg Opinion*. Strain is frequently interviewed by major media outlets, speaks often to a variety of audiences, and has testified before Congress. He holds a PhD in economics from Cornell University and lives in Washington, DC.